"Through her most vulnerable writing, Ruth Graham shares with us the topic of forgiveness. In this encouraging book, she incorporates her own personal experiences as well as biblical Scripture to help guide us as readers to a better understanding of what forgiveness means and why we should choose forgiveness."

Mark Batterson, *New York Times* bestselling author of *The Circle Maker* and lead pastor of National Community Church

"*Forgiving My Father, Forgiving Myself* is an honest, heart-felt, and insightful book about the power of forgiveness. Through the lens of her own life journey, Ruth Graham shares biblical principles of forgiveness that can truly liberate even the most broken relationships. I am grateful for her vulnerability and courage to write such a book."

Sean McDowell, PhD, Biola University professor, speaker, and author

"This transparent, readable, and life-changing book is one you will not be able to put down once you start reading it. You will buy copies for your friends. You will thank God for Ruth Graham and Romans 8:28—that all things 'work together for good' to those who love God."

Dr. R. T. Kendall

"I know of no Christian communicator more transparent, vulnerable, honest, and encouraging in our shared Christian walk than Ruth Graham. Her genuine love of Jesus, her family, and the family of God inspires us to follow her in authenticity, confession, compassion, and commitment. Ruth is a faithful, prayerful, trusted guide through life's trials and through God's Word, helping us find our way home through forgiveness. Writing from personal experience, reliance upon Scripture, and divine guidance from the Holy Spirit, Ruth has given us the forgiveness book-of-the-year!"

Randall O'Brien, president of Carson-Newman University, 2008–18, and author of *Set Free by Forgiveness: The Way to Peace and Healing*

FORGIVING *My Father,* FORGIVING *Myself*

An Invitation to the Miracle of Forgiveness

RUTH GRAHAM
with Cindy Lambert

BakerBooks

a division of Baker Publishing Group
Grand Rapids, Michigan

© 2019 by Ruth Graham

Published by Baker Books
a division of Baker Publishing Group
PO Box 6287, Grand Rapids, MI 49516-6287
www.bakerbooks.com

Printed in the United States of America

Library of Congress Cataloging-in-Publication Data
Names: Graham, Ruth, 1950- author.
Title: Forgiving my father, forgiving myself : an invitation to the miracle of forgiveness / Ruth Graham, with Cindy Lambert.
Description: Grand Rapids : Baker Books, a division of Baker Publishing Group, 2019. | Includes bibliographical references
Identifiers: LCCN 2019017282 | ISBN 9780801094262 (cloth : alk. paper)
Subjects: LCSH: Forgiveness—Religious aspects—Christianity.
Classification: LCC BV4647.F55 G73 2019 | DDC 234/.5—dc23
LC record available at https://lccn.loc.gov/2019017282)

978-0-8010-9464-4 (ITPE)

Unless otherwise indicated, Scripture quotations are from the New American Standard Bible® (NASB), copyright © 1960, 1962, 1963, 1968, 1971, 1972, 1973, 1975, 1977, 1995 by The Lockman Foundation. Used by permission. www.Lockman.org

Scripture quotations labeled ASV are from the American Standard Version of the Bible.

Scripture quotations labeled Message are from THE MESSAGE, copyright © 1993, 1994, 1995, 1996, 2000, 2001, 2002 by Eugene H. Peterson. Used by permission of NavPress. All rights reserved. Represented by Tyndale House Publishers, Inc.

Scripture quotations labeled NIV are from the Holy Bible, New International Version®. NIV®. Copyright © 1973, 1978, 1984, 2011 by Biblica, Inc.™ Used by permission of Zondervan. All rights reserved worldwide. www.zondervan.com. The "NIV" and "New International Version" are trademarks registered in the United States Patent and Trademark Office by Biblica, Inc.™

Scripture quotations labeled NLT are from the Holy Bible, New Living Translation, copyright © 1996, 2004, 2007, 2013, 2015 by Tyndale House Foundation. Used by permission of Tyndale House Publishers, Inc., Carol Stream, Illinois 60188. All rights reserved.

The author is represented by Ambassador Literary Agency, Nashville, Tennessee.

Some names and identifying details have been changed to protect the privacy of individuals.

19 20 21 22 23 24 25   7 6 5 4 3 2 1

In keeping with biblical principles of creation stewardship, Baker Publishing Group advocates the responsible use of our natural resources. As a member of the Green Press Initiative, our company uses recycled paper when possible. The text paper of this book is composed in part of post-consumer waste.

For my children, Noelle, Graham,
and Windsor, whose forgiveness is unmeasured.

The most influential person in your life is the one you have not forgiven.

Anonymous

Contents

ONE

Beyond the Prison Walls

> If we cooperate with Him in loving obedience, God
> will manifest Himself to us, and that manifestation
> will be the difference between a nominal Christian life
> and a life radiant with the light of His face.
>
> A. W. Tozer

"Can I sing you a song?" the young man said, his eager
brown eyes meeting mine with a gentleness that took
me by surprise. The thought of music in the dismal setting of
death row at Angola Prison in Louisiana seemed incongru-
ous but was also a welcome relief. I doubt if he knew how
nervous I was, but his kindness and openness helped put
me at ease. I had intended to be the one to bring a measure
of comfort and encouragement to him, but he seemed to be
reversing our roles.

"Yes, thank you, Michael." I knew only his first name and
that he was awaiting his upcoming execution. I didn't know

the crime or crimes that brought him here. I didn't know his story, nor did he know mine other than that I was a daughter of Billy Graham, visiting his prison with a ministry team. We'd met only moments before over a handshake, his small brown hand extended through the bars between us.

Michael, maybe in his thirties, was short, with dark hair and an open face. He stepped closer to the bars, took a deep breath, and with eyes warm and kind he began to sing a cappella.

"When peace, like a river, attendeth my way," he began.[1]

His rich baritone voice filled the austere confines of his cell and echoed down the concrete hallway behind me. Tears filled my eyes. Though I knew the words well, I'd never heard them sung by a man condemned to soon die.

"It is well . . ." He began the chorus softly, like a gentle whisper. "With my soul." He held the note, his voice strong and steady, then, as if he were releasing all the passion in his heart, his voice opened wide and full. "It is well, it is well, with my soul."

And I knew it was.

The conviction in his voice, the peace on his face, told me all was well in the soul of this man. I could not speak. I was overwhelmed by the powerful grace of God. Michael and I both knew that in spite of the steel and concrete between him and the outside world, in spite of the execution date looming before him, he was at peace with his God. Whatever had brought him here had been forgiven. This man's spirit was free and secure in his redemption. He was my brother in Christ. When he finished he stepped back with a soft smile.

My time with him was short. I had only a few minutes with each prisoner. I suggested we pray together, and then came another surprise.

"Before you go, I have something I'd like to give you," he said. Again, I felt our roles had been reversed. What gift could this imprisoned man possibly have for me? His barren cell had nothing but a bed with a thin mattress, a pillow, and a small unit that provided a metal toilet and sink. He walked over to his bed, reached beneath the covers, and pulled out something small. He stepped back toward me, took my hand through the bars, and placed in my palm a small woven cloth cross. "I wove this from threads of my bedsheets. I'd like you to have it."

I saw how fine the threads were, how intricately hand-woven, and wondered how many hours it had taken him to make it. The gift touched my heart. Tears were so close it was difficult to speak.

"It's a precious gift, Michael. Thank you." We held hands, prayed together, and said goodbye. I was sad our time was so brief. I would have loved to visit with him longer, but I had to move on, so I stepped away, on to the next cell, feeling I'd just been on holy ground. I knew I'd never see Michael again and assumed the story of our brief encounter had ended.

I never dreamed that Michael's story and mine had another chapter to come, a chapter that would challenge me to begin to rethink what I thought I knew about forgiveness.

Living Condemned, Yet Free

Angola Prison, the Louisiana State Penitentiary where each prisoner is serving a life sentence, seems an unlikely place to spark new thoughts and a deeper understanding of forgiveness. It is, after all, a place where every prisoner has to pay the earthly consequences of their crimes. Every one of the over six thousand inmates (except in a few very rare exceptions) would die within its confines—some by execution, others by old age or illness or injury.

Burl Cain, the warden, had invited Ruth Graham & Friends, the ministry God had given to me, to minister to the inmates on this particular weekend and had allowed the press to chronicle our visit. I had accepted the invitation to the swamp-surrounded prison grounds months before, with confidence the gospel of Jesus Christ could make a huge difference in the lives of the inmates. I confess that before meeting Michael, as I passed all the razor wire and walked the long concrete corridor to death row, my footsteps echoing in the stifling atmosphere, I worried that I was inadequate for the job. After all, what did I—a middle-aged homemaker and grandmother—have to say that could make a difference in the lives of what I assumed were hardened criminals? In fact, in the moment I first heard the great steel gates clang shut behind me upon entering death row that day, my only thought was a sick feeling of inadequacy and anxiety that embarrassed me. I tried to quiet my rattled emotions by reminding myself that I was safe, and my stay was only temporary. I was acutely aware that such thoughts were not the stuff of a victorious spiritual moment.

My nervousness made me all the more grateful for my traveling companions—the wonderful team of dedicated men and women who shared in the ministry of Ruth Graham & Friends. We were used to traveling together to minister all over the country and beyond, from an ice-hockey stadium in Canada to city auditoriums, churches, and retreat centers— wherever the Lord opened doors for us to cover topics that often weren't discussed in many churches. Each member of the team had an area of expertise: a psychologist who spoke on depression, another on domestic abuse, a minister who spoke of his experience recovering from addiction to pornography, a woman who shared her recovery from abortion and another her recovery from drug addiction. All of them had more experience in prison ministry than me, but none of us were prison ministry experts.

When we reached death row, our team split up so we could go cell to cell and speak individually with as many prisoners as possible. I was uneasy. I have always reacted negatively to the idea of people in cages. As a young woman, I went as part of a church ministry team to a local prison. The sight of lovely young women behind bars haunted me. I talked and laughed with them, related to them, and prayed with them. Later I found out that the woman I'd seemed to connect with the most was a murderer, and I promptly decided I was probably not called to prison ministry! Clearly, as I now stood on death row, God was causing me to rethink that conclusion, showing me that it was His power and presence, not mine, that made a difference in hearts and souls.

After meeting Michael, I heard others' stories through ears newly opened to the reality that we weren't bringing God with us but rather were meeting Him already there, at work in powerful ways. No longer concerned about my inadequacy, I was able to see God's power at work—something so evident that day. I met men at every level of faith: some who wanted nothing to do with us and turned their backs, some curious about God, some hungry to hear of God's love for them, some eager to share their faith stories with me, and some men of great faith, humbled by brokenness yet who appeared healed and whole. When we led worship with the inmates, we were overwhelmed with the power of thanksgiving and rejoicing we witnessed. So many of these prisoners were living in true freedom.

How had they done it? How had they accepted God's forgiveness for the wrongs they had done? (I had trouble doing that for myself.) How had they forgiven themselves? (A major struggle for me.) How had they forgiven the many who had wronged them along their painful journeys? (My journey paled in comparison to the pain many of them had known.) I couldn't imagine. When we left, I took those questions with me, determined to seek answers from God. My moments with Michael, in particular, stayed on my heart. He'd left me with the powerful image of a man whose soul was well and whose spirit was free.

Michael's Reunion

Some months after my visit to Angola Prison, I received an email from a man who had read on the internet about our team's visit to death row. He asked me if I had met a prisoner there named Michael. He gave a last name as well, but I'd not been given the last names of any of the prisoners. Our team had met with many men. I had no idea how many Michaels may have been among them.

He wrote that the Michael of interest to him was scheduled to die, and he wanted to know if he was a believer. Did he know Jesus? He didn't tell me his own story or why he wanted to know, but I hoped he meant the young man who sang so movingly. The only way to know was for me to call the warden.

So I called Burl Cain, who told me that, indeed, it was the same man.

"He's scheduled for execution at the end of this month, Ruth," he said. "Michael has professed his faith in Jesus and is assured of his salvation." Such a mix of sadness and joy stirred in me. I was sad that Michael's death was near but joyful that eternity with Jesus awaited him.

I emailed the man to assure him that Michael's relationship with Christ was secure. "May I ask," I wrote, "why you are interested in this particular young man?"

He wrote back that Michael had murdered his young grandson in a horrific way. He went on to explain that he had forgiven Michael years ago and had been praying for his salvation ever since. He said he took no pleasure in the young man's impending execution and wanted to make sure he was going to heaven. Then he told me he was a missionary in Nepal.

Over eight thousand miles away! I marveled at the grace of God at work through the technology that allowed this missionary in Nepal to know about my visit to a particular murderer in Louisiana. But more, I marveled at this missionary's forgiveness.

I was a grandmother myself and shuddered at the thought of one of my precious grandchildren being brutally murdered. I was amazed that this man cared about his grandson's murderer so much that he was compelled to reach out in love across the years and the continents.

Forgiveness broke the power of the evil deed. Forgiveness broke down the distance and the time. Forgiveness overcame his sorrow. It penetrated the cement walls and prison bars into death row, and it celebrated that Michael's eternal

15

judgment and penalty for murder had been paid by Jesus. Michael was a man society had forgotten and written off, but neither God nor this grandfather of a murdered child had forgotten him or written him off. He was redeemed by the blood of Jesus. He would be welcomed into heaven with joy! And his story would live on to have a lasting impact.

This is far more than a touching story to me. It is personal. For not only had I walked death row and heard the sweet voice of this imprisoned brother in Christ raised in song but I had a handwoven cross hanging in my home as a reminder that I'd witnessed the power of forgiveness that had penetrated the prison walls of Angola and transformed a once-hardened heart. I wanted that power to penetrate my own life in new ways. I wanted to personally experience *that* depth of freedom that comes with forgiveness. For when it came to grace and forgiveness, both Michael and the missionary in Nepal knew a freedom I longed for in my own life.

Michael was executed later that month, but I'm sure that, as he stepped into heaven, a little boy was there to greet him. They had a reunion, not as victim and murderer but as sons of the living God. And I rejoice that this boy's grandfather one day will join them with a song in his heart. Three souls will gather in heaven as forgiven saints redeemed by the blood of Jesus. Only forgiveness by God's grace can do that! And that, to me, is miraculous, for such life transformation can only take place by the power of God.

Could I have done the same as this grandfather? I'll be honest—it is hard to imagine. Certainly not in my own power. I have suffered wrongs far less tragic and devastating and have found it a struggle to forgive so completely. Forgiveness has not come easily to me, in spite of my resolute desire to exercise it. I've struggled to forgive those who have wounded me. I've struggled even more to forgive myself. And I confess I've even struggled—and this is not pretty— with the question of forgiving God for seemingly failing to meet some of my own personal expectations. I've paid a price for my lack of forgiveness. I've tasted bitterness and the desire for revenge. I've lost sleep and relationships. I've sacrificed peace and my own well-being. I've run up against the narrow limits of my love and found myself feeling any- thing but patient and kind and filled with grace. I've wanted to punish myself; I've wanted to see others punished. Need I go on?

I know I am not alone in my struggle with forgiveness.

As I travel to minister on the topics of betrayal, abuse, loss, and suffering, I hear the heart cries of so many who want to find their way through anger, bitterness, and resentment to the freedom of forgiveness. Countless numbers of believers know firsthand the hard struggle of trying to forgive, only to be knocked down by emotions and memories. They are confronted by anger, revenge, bitterness, judgment, or the self-condemnation of shame. I know what it is to believe I have forgiven only to be surprised when my wounds are trig- gered and I am left to fight the battle all over again.

But I *want* forgiveness to rule in my heart! I want, like that missionary in Nepal, to pray wholeheartedly for the life and well-being and eternal peace and goodness of those who have wronged me. I want to look in the mirror and see a woman at peace with life and those around her, one who sees herself standing before God clothed in Jesus's righ- teousness and therefore blameless. I want to look at those who have wronged me and see not what wrongs they have committed but see them as God sees them: covered by His love and grace. The same way He sees me! I want to look to my heavenly Father and see not my unmet expectations and disappointments but His perfect loving will at work in my life. I want to trust Him so fully that I rest in His power and love, knowing that He chooses only the very best for my life, even when I cannot yet comprehend it.

From Knowledge to Transformation

There are so many books on the subject of forgiveness already on the market—some classic, some practical, some psychological, some theological. My library shelves are filled with them. Many are excellent. Why, then, do I believe we need another book on the subject? Because forgiveness is the very heart of God—it is the very reason that Jesus came to earth. For those of us who wrestle to have our *head knowledge* about forgiveness transformed into the *life-changing experience* of forgiveness, the subject is worthy of our continued exploration.

Different books touch different lives for different reasons. I'm grateful for the many books that have helped shape my understanding and my experience of forgiveness. I've been challenged, informed, surprised, and influenced by so many—even maddened, frustrated, and ultimately convicted by some. One thing I discovered is that, for me, pat answers didn't cut it. I wanted to work through the subject with someone who knew what I was experiencing, someone who would be transparent enough to tell it like it is—the good, the bad, and the ugly. I needed someone to be real about the struggle and personal journey they experienced. I came to a point where I didn't need a forgiveness handbook nor a sermon nor a biblical treatise. I wanted to know how others handled it and to learn if my struggle was a valid one. I wanted some company on my journey so that I could know I was not alone. I couldn't seem to find that book, so I've written it.

In my very deliberate and intentional journey toward forgiveness, I have had some profound experiences—both giving and receiving it. I fought hard through the concept, wrestling with God every step of the way. I had to face up to the fact that sometimes I didn't want to forgive. I thought by forgiving I was letting "them" off the hook. My wounds were deep. My pain was real. Forgiveness was a gift I thought some didn't deserve, and it seemed it required me to pay for it whether I forgave or not. Like the sign in the store, "If you break it you buy it," I felt I had to pay the price of giving forgiveness even if I wasn't the one who "broke it." I also had to be honest that at times I wanted "them" to hurt as much as I did or to feel the same level of pain they had inflicted on me. Like a wounded animal, more than once I even lashed out and hurt those who tried to help.

I have also argued with God over the idea of asking others for forgiveness. I didn't want to do it. Wasn't I justified in what I did? Didn't they deserve what they got? Why should I ask their forgiveness? What if they used it against me? I wasn't the one who did wrong, was I? Did I really have to go to them? Isn't it better just to let it go? But I discovered it didn't let *me* go!

And then there are the wounds buried deep inside, long forgotten until something triggers a memory and they come roaring back, front and center. Such memories can throw us for a loop and leave us either sorting through emotions we don't want to feel or scrambling to rebury them. What would it be like to face them head-on and have forgiveness win the day?

At times my pain was visceral. I couldn't even look at the pain to examine it. I just wanted out of it. But that was not going to happen. I had to go through the suffering. I could go through it my way and end up bitter and hardened, or I could do it God's way, being molded more into Jesus's image. Did I trust God enough to push through the pain?

Do you?

My ultimate goal in all my wrestling with forgiveness is to be more like Him. Taking my wounds to Jesus is the only way I can accomplish it.

In this book, you will read some of my journey through forgiveness—it isn't neat or tidy or smooth. Far from it. Neither is this a "tell-all" of any kind. But it is my personal and honest story, telling how God has been with me the whole way. Now that I've emerged with a far richer experience of forgiveness, I don't want to keep it to myself. I want to share it! I want to come alongside others who also struggle and let them know that they are not alone. There is hope. There is freedom.

Do I have it down? No. Not by a long shot. But I hope in these pages to challenge misunderstandings of the nature of forgiveness, to stimulate deeper longings for authentic forgiveness, and to help break through roadblocks that keep us trapped in the broken cycles of unforgiveness. I want to invite you to experience the miracle that occurs when forgiveness pours from the heart of God and washes over you and through you. Let's refuse to surrender on forgiveness until we, like Michael, are no longer held prisoner but are free to enjoy all that forgiveness has to offer.

One thing I have learned that is absolutely true: such forgiveness is a *process*. A *lifelong* process. I won't have it buttoned up until I am in heaven. Until then, I keep going through the process while leaning on God's outrageous grace.

Lean with me.

TWO

Forgiveness Isn't Fair

To be a Christian means to forgive the inexcusable because God has forgiven the inexcusable in you.

C. S. Lewis

When I was a girl of about eleven, my family spent the
better part of our summer in Switzerland, thanks to
the generosity of others. My father had many engagements
in Europe that season. My two older sisters, two younger
brothers, and I were accustomed to many long separations
from our father as he traveled the globe preaching the gospel,
and I always missed him terribly, so I was as excited as my
four siblings that we'd all have a good part of this particular
summer together as a family.

It was our practice as a family to gather for devotions
at least once a day, usually twice. One morning, one of my
younger brothers had been teasing me mercilessly. He kept
hitting me, then running away. Of course, as the irritated

23

older sister, I would hit him back while yelling, "Stop it!" This went on for some time that morning, my irritation growing. Mother told us to stop, and when it came time for devotions, she sat between us to prevent further incidents. But, as little brothers often are, my brother was persistently aggravating. Time and time again, when no one was looking, he would reach around Mother's back and poke me. Naturally, I'd reach around too and poke him back. This went on for a bit, and then my father stepped in and sternly told us to quit. We were to settle down and be quiet. Devotions proceeded.

I thought at first that Daddy's words had stopped the torture. Not so. After a few minutes, my brother reached around Mother's back and poked me again. This time, I reached in front of her and hit him back. My father saw me—I was caught!

Daddy was aggravated by this time. He got up and grabbed me, put me over his knee, and spanked me for disobeying, ignoring my pleas that my brother had hit me first! That would have been humiliating enough had only my family been present, but it so happened that family friends were present as well. I'm sure I turned ten shades of scarlet, utterly embarrassed. To be punished by my father was a great rarity. I was a compliant child, usually eager to please, and my heart broke over this crushing punishment that, as far as I was concerned, was unfair as I saw my brother, not myself, as guilty.

When the spanking was over, I wanted to run to my room, but my father held me fast in his arms as I struggled to get away. He told me he loved me but that I had disobeyed him and so was punished. At that moment, I didn't hear it. I wouldn't hear it. (Interestingly, when I look back today on how my father held me close after the spanking, I see that he was holding me close to his father-heart out of his tender love for me while teaching me a hard lesson. My, how time can change one's perspective!) It seemed so unfair. What about my brother? He suffered no consequences at all. Was I just supposed to forgive him and let it go? To my mind it was totally unfair that my brother got away with being the initiator while I paid the price for responding as I had.

That was over fifty years ago. Obviously, I still remember it. What's more, I recall not only the incident but my powerful feelings of humiliation and unfairness. The shame. The anger. I remember feeling that it wouldn't have been so bad if my brother had been spanked too. Unfairness, whether real or perceived, is hard to bear and challenging to forgive.

Of course, this is a relatively insignificant event compared to the wounds I later suffered in life or those that so many people carry. But big or small, we can all relate to the heart cry, "That's not fair!" It's not fair that some "get away" with their deeds while we pay a price. No one taught us to feel this way; it just comes naturally. How many times have you said, "That's not fair," or at least thought it? If you are a parent, how many times have you had that statement lobbed at you? And how many times have you replied, "Too bad. Life is unfair."

Where do we get the notion that life should be fair? Bedtime stories and fairy tales, where the good guys live happily ever after and the villains get their due, underscore the innate sense that bad guys should get punished and good guys should win. It seems so satisfying when everyone gets an equal share of what's coming to them. But I believe the

25

yearning for fairness runs far deeper in our souls than that. I believe that the intrinsic value of fairness was imprinted on our souls by God, who is always just. We are born with it. Just as we were created to love God and enjoy Him forever, so we were created for life in the garden—a perfect life in constant communion with our perfect and just God. But sin changed all that. Injustice entered the world, and with it our innate sense of fairness was violated.

So, let's lay it out there and acknowledge it: life *is* unfair. Forgiveness is *not* fair.

Simply put, the scales are never balanced on this spinning planet. I validate the common observation that often the good suffer while the evil flourish. God's Word confirms this as well. David often bemoaned this reality, as he wrote,

> For I was envious of the arrogant
> As I saw the prosperity of the wicked.
> For there are no pains in their death,
> And their body is fat. (Ps. 73:3–4)

And Jeremiah felt that same sting as he pleaded with God,

> Righteous are You, O LORD, that I would plead my
>   case with You;
> Indeed I would discuss matters of justice with You:
> Why has the way of the wicked prospered?
> Why are all those who deal in treachery at ease? (Jer.
>   12:1)

It's not our imagination. Those who wrong us sometimes get away with it, and we end up paying the price. This offends our strong sense of fairness—at least when it comes to being on the "right" side of the equation. And somehow, don't we usually find ourselves on the right side? Funny how that always seems to happen—the perception of being on the right side—to those on *both* sides of an incident!

The Question of Innocence

Of course, there is one fatal flaw in such thinking, one critical detail we tend to overlook when we yearn for life to be fair. Paul told us simply,

> What then? Are we better than they? Not at all . . . "There is none righteous, not even one." (Rom. 3:9–10)

And therein lies the problem with our longing for fairness: none of us get it right. Every one of us is guilty of sin before God. We may prefer to look at others, at those who wrong us, as *more* guilty, *more* sinful, but the fact is sin is sin is sin. Finger-pointing is useless when we realize that seeing the sins of others is nothing more than looking at a mirror of our own misdeeds.

Still, even understanding that truth intellectually doesn't remove our yearning for justice—and our resistance to forgiveness—when we are wronged, does it?

Is the betrayed spouse to forgive the adulterous one?

Is the intimidated worker to forgive the bullying boss?

Is the falsely accused defendant to forgive the lying accuser?

27

Is the betrayed friend to forgive the trusted confidant
who betrayed that trust?

Is the conscientious employee to forgive the unjust
supervisor?

Is the sexually abused teen to forgive the abuser?

The simple answer to each of these complex scenarios
is yes.

Before you slam this book shut, hold on! We are going
to unpack such complicated questions. We will distinguish
between forgiveness and trust, forgiveness and reconciliation, forgiveness and continuing victimization. Such issues
are critically important to understand.

For now, however, recall your own list of wrongs done
to you, the pain of the injustice, the consequences you've
suffered. This isn't a philosophical discussion, is it? No. It's
not. It's practical. It's real. Forgiveness often *feels* unfair, like
we are letting someone off the hook for an injury against us.
We fear it means they will not have to pay for what they did.
The scale of justice seems unbalanced. Even when it comes
to forgiving ourselves, it is hard to let ourselves off the hook.
Forgiveness causes a struggle when we are confronted with a
deep wrong that left a gaping wound in our heart, a wound
that we know we *should* forgive but don't feel we have it in
us to do so. We have tried, but the feelings of hurt, shame,
anger, and bitterness come back, unbidden, and sink us like
a stone.

We make excuses for ourselves and justify our feelings. We
try to forgive, and it doesn't feel good, it doesn't last, or we
still feel the pain of it, and we remember, *But they . . .* Yes,

there are all kinds of excuses to not forgive. I once heard Dr. Vance Havner, an old Southern country preacher, say, "An excuse is a skin of a reason stuffed with a lie." A wise man once told me, "Love doesn't make excuses. Love forgives." And I think I'd add, love doesn't accept excuses, it calls for responsibility. The responsibility to forgive is hard and becomes a struggle. How do we get beyond that struggle?

Such struggle is the reality for those of us who feel stuck in unforgiveness. How do we get unstuck? The pain, the grief, and the price we pay are powerfully real. Even when we *want* to forgive (and often we don't really want to at all), we seem unable to muster up the wherewithal to actually do it. It's not easy. Forgiveness comes at a terribly high price.

Peter must have had the same struggle. He asked Jesus a question: "Lord, how often shall my brother sin against me and I forgive him? Up to seven times?" (Matt. 18:21). We are not told what prompted Peter to ask the question. Perhaps he had a specific person in mind. A family member who continued to put him down? A neighbor who kept taking advantage? A friend who had broken a trust? We aren't told. Or perhaps Peter was thinking of himself. Maybe his impulsiveness got him into trouble more than once, and he kept needing to be forgiven. (I know the Bible doesn't tell us these things . . . I am using my imagination.) Whatever prompted him, this was something Peter wanted to find out. So he asked Jesus if forgiving seven times was satisfactory. The rabbis of the day taught that three times was sufficient, so Peter doubled that and threw in one more for good measure. Going above and beyond—so like Peter.

I am sure each of us has asked a similar question, hoping that Jesus's response might give us some wiggle room. We'd like to think there is a point at which the transgression is so grievous that we don't have to forgive. I remember recently talking with an older gentleman who told me, "Some things cannot be forgiven." I wasn't sure what deep hurt was in his heart, but I ached for him. However, Jesus's answer doesn't give us any wiggle room. Not only that but His answer goes beyond imagination: "Jesus said to him, 'I do not say to you, up to seven times, but up to seventy times seven'" (v. 22). Wow! That's over the top! What He is saying is that we are to model God's character in our response to an offense. That's tough. Yet it is the standard for which we are to strive.

So, if we are to actually model God's character in response to an offense, what does that "seventy times seven" actually look like? We don't have to wonder. God has already drawn us a picture, in living color. And He has demonstrated that He knows far better than we how unfair forgiveness really is. He knows how high the cost.

The Picture of Forgiveness

It began with a kiss. The kiss of a friend.

Perhaps you, like me, have heard the story so many times that your senses have been dulled to it. Take a fresh look with me.

> While He was still speaking, behold, Judas, one of the twelve, came up accompanied by a large crowd with swords and clubs, who came from the chief priests and elders of the people. . . . Immediately Judas went to Jesus and said, "Hail, Rabbi!" and kissed Him. And Jesus said to him, "Friend, do

what you have come for." Then they came and laid hands on Jesus and seized Him. (Matt. 26:47, 49–50)

I am struck by the gentleness of the moment. Jesus didn't run. He didn't struggle. He didn't even condemn His betrayer. What did He do? He focused the attention of His captors on the power of God Almighty.

And behold, one of those who were with Jesus reached and drew out his sword, and struck the slave of the high priest and cut off his ear. Then Jesus said to him, "Put your sword back into its place; for all those who take up the sword shall perish by the sword. Or do you think that I cannot appeal to My Father, and He will at once put at My disposal more than twelve legions of angels?" (vv. 51–53)

Then He displayed God's power by healing the man's ear!

To leave no doubt that submitting peacefully to the mock trial and tortuous death was a willing and purposeful act on His part, He spelled it out clearly for all to hear: "But all this has taken place to fulfill the Scriptures of the prophets" (v. 56). His focus was on His purpose. He had "set His face" for this in order to pay the price for my sin and yours.

Jesus went peacefully to appear before the high priest, where He endured false testimony and accusations as well as arrogant questions and insinuations.

But Jesus kept silent. And the high priest said to Him, "I adjure You by the living God, that You tell us whether You are the Christ, the Son of God." Jesus said to him, "You have said it yourself; nevertheless I tell you, hereafter you will see the Son of Man sitting at the right hand of Power, and coming on the clouds of heaven." (vv. 63–64)

He left no doubt in their minds as to who He was and the position awaiting Him in heaven, knowing full well what would follow.

Then they spat in His face and beat Him with their fists; and others slapped Him, and said, "Prophesy to us, You Christ; who is the one who hit You?" (vv. 67–68)

Even as He was suffering this physical assault, emotionally He was also being assaulted by His dear friend. He knew that His passionate disciple, Peter, one of His inner circle, was outside in the courtyard, denying even knowing Him. Next, He stood before the governor, Pilate, and heard the fateful question posed to His own people: "Which of the two do you want me to release for you?" (27:21).

He knew what their answer would be, these very people who only one week before had been shouting "Hosanna" and waving palm branches.

And they said, "Barabbas." Pilate said to them, "Then what shall I do with Jesus who is called Christ?" They all said, "Crucify Him!" And he said, "Why, what evil has He done?" But they kept shouting all the more, saying, "Crucify Him!" (vv. 21–23)

I think about Jesus's three years of exhausting selfless ministry, His teaching and traveling and healing and loving. I cannot fathom the sense of betrayal He must have felt. The emotional pain. He even knew that what came next would not only tear at His heart but at His flesh and bones.

Jesus was stripped of His clothes and tied with His arms above His head so the whole of His back was exposed. A Roman soldier, trained for battle, strong and rested, beat Jesus with a flagrum—a short whip made of several heavy leather strips imbedded with lead balls. The soldier used his full strength to bring the whip against Jesus's bared back, shoulders, and legs. At first it produced bruises, then it cut the skin, and with each blow it cut deeper and deeper, exposing muscles and blood vessels until the skin was hanging in ribbons. Jesus's back was unrecognizable as a human's. When the Roman soldier determined that Jesus was near death due to blood loss and exhaustion, the beating stopped. Jesus was untied, and He collapsed to the blood-wet ground.

Then the sadistic Roman soldiers made fun of Jesus. They threw a robe over His shoulders and made a crown of thorns and jammed it into His scalp. They mocked Him, saying, "Hail to the King of the Jews." They put the rough wooden crossbeam on His bruised, raw, bloody shoulder and made Him begin the arduous, agonizing walk up to Golgotha where He would be crucified.

Yet, with every step He took, Jesus knew He was accomplishing His purpose.

> But He was pierced through for our transgressions,
> He was crushed for our iniquities;
> The chastening for our well-being fell upon Him,
> And by His scourging we are healed.
> All of us like sheep have gone astray,
> Each of us has turned to his own way;

But the LORD has caused the iniquity of us all
To fall on Him. (Isa. 53:5–6)

The Romans had crucifixion—one of the cruelest means of execution ever invented—down to a science. The words of Dr. Truman Davis help me better understand the depths of suffering that Jesus endured.

[The cross-beam is placed on the ground and] Jesus [is] quickly thrown backward with His shoulders against the wood. The legionnaire feels for the depression at the front of the wrist. He drives a heavy, square, wrought-iron nail through the wrist and deep into the wood. Quickly, he moves to the other side and repeats the action, being careful not to pull the arms too tightly, but to allow some flexion and movement. . . .

The left foot is now pressed backward against the right foot, and with both feet extended, toes down, a nail is driven through the arch of each, leaving the knees moderately flexed. The Victim is now crucified. As He slowly sags down with more weight on the nails in the wrists, excruciating pain shoots along the fingers and up the arms to explode in the brain. . . .

As He pushes Himself up to avoid this stretching torment, He places His full weight on the nail through His feet. Again there is the searing agony of the nail tearing through the nerves . . . great waves of cramps sweep over the muscles, knotting them in deep, relentless, throbbing pain. With these cramps comes the inability to push Himself upward. Hanging by His arms, the pectoral muscles are paralyzed. . . . Air can be drawn into the lungs, but cannot be exhaled. Jesus fights to raise Himself in order to get even one short breath.[1]

And then He used that precious, painful breath to say, "Father, forgive them; for they do not know what they are doing" (Luke 23:34).

There is no question about it; forgiveness isn't fair. It is a generous gift beyond imagination, bought and paid for by the blood of Jesus Christ. Freely and willingly and purposely given to those who don't deserve it. Like me. Like you.

Forgiveness isn't fair. It is holy!

THREE

God's Heartbeat

Forgiveness is ultimately a form of love, a love that
accepts others as they are.

Dr. David Stoop ·

I was thirty-six years old when I began my first real wrestling match with forgiveness.

Not to say I'd never encountered the need to forgive and
be forgiven before that. I'd certainly had my share of hurts
and caused others hurt as well. Who hasn't? But my understanding of forgiveness before that point was, I see now, fairly
elementary. I didn't yet understand the essence of forgiveness.
I thought it was all about feelings. And since I was a master
at masking my negative feelings, even from myself, whenever
I encountered a need to give forgiveness I'd been satisfied to
pray, meditate on some forgiveness verses, and then do my
best to forget my pain. I believed the old saying that "time
heals all wounds."

Little did I know that, in truth, time *buries* all wounds that are not dealt with, and such wounds are buried alive. So, buried they remained, securely tucked away beneath my layers of denial and repression until I experienced a life-altering trauma—one that shook me to my core and threatened to tear off my well-worn mask. Suddenly, I found my understanding of forgiveness wholly inadequate, and I floundered.

That trauma began when I learned that my husband of eighteen years had been unfaithful. Not once or twice, but multiple times over a period of years. It was then that all those old, living wounds began to reach out of their graves and grab me when I was least able to deal with them. Eventually (much later) I would learn that I would have to open all those graves and bring my wounds one by one into the light of God's forgiveness. But that's another chapter.

I'd love to report that, in the wake of learning of my husband's infidelity, I kept my head clear and my heart wise, but I did neither. Instead, I found myself spiraling into a period of confusion and pain, and though I reached in desperation for God's way through the storm, I suffered dreadfully and made a series of poor decisions that not only hurt me but hurt my children as well. Anger, rage, hurt, and despair wreaked havoc in my heart. My new brokenness revealed my old, hidden brokenness. Life got extremely messy; I was a mess, and I made a mess. Fortunately, we are loved by a God who transforms messes into messages. For me that is not just a clever turn of words. I am intensely grateful for the message He's been writing in and through my life since the beginning, even in my messiest of times.

I told much of that experience and its aftermath in my book *In Every Pew Sits a Broken Heart.* By the end of that book I revealed two subsequent marriages that ended in divorce—one that lasted a mere three months, and one that lasted for almost ten years. To this day, praise God, I receive the most amazing messages from readers who share their stories of restoration and growth and healing sparked by their reading of that book. I am in awe. Only our grace-filled God would use such a leaky broken vessel as me to carry His message of love and restoration to others.

I am so thankful for the Word of God, which has shown me that I'm in good company, for there we can see God at work through a murderer such as Moses, an adulterer such as King David, a prostitute such as Rahab, a betrayer such as Peter, and a persecutor of Christians such as Saul, who later became the apostle Paul. Clearly, God uses broken, messy people to do His work, and in the process He restores and heals them. God is masterful in redeeming the broken, and the practice of forgiveness plays a huge part in that redemption. In our culture *broken* usually means useless, ready to be thrown away. Not in God's economy. Brokenness qualifies us for His service.

For me, forgiveness is not some lofty theological concept to intellectually contemplate. It is the healing and restoration I had craved for years. Whether I am throwing myself at the mercy seat of God, struggling to forgive myself for my failures, willfulness, and sin, or wrestling with God to forgive someone I believe wronged me, forgiveness is an absolute necessity in my Christian walk. I know what it is to thirst for forgiveness; I have pursued it with passion, I have stretched to lay hold of it, and I have melted into the arms of God, restored because of it.

You need to know up front that I'm not proud of my brokenness. I am, however, grateful that God is using it in writing the story of His grace and forgiveness. Unlike years ago at the dissolution of my first marriage, when I wanted to hide myself and my pain and my flaws away from the eyes of the world, I know since the writing of *In Every Pew Sits a Broken Heart* that God calls me to use my story for His work and glory. When I do, I discover that He uses it as an encouragement to others who feel broken, wounded, betrayed, and in need of forgiving and being forgiven, so within these pages I will dip into my own experiences with forgiveness in addition to the stories of others, who've granted their permission, and, of course, we will explore God's Word for direction and wisdom.

An Apprentice of Forgiveness

I am not writing this book as a forgiveness expert but as a recipient, and not as a forgiveness master but as an apprentice. I like that image because the whole concept of an apprenticeship is on-the-job training by a master craftsperson. How fitting! For in my ongoing journey, forgiveness has been learned through instruction from the Master through His Word, then through trial and error and practice and failure and more practice. Along the way God has also provided me some great teachers such as Dr. R. T. Kendall, Dr. Randall O'Brien, Dr. Lewis B. Smedes, and others whom I'll be quoting in these pages. I've been discovering what forgiveness is and what it is not, its ultimate purpose, the power to persevere through it, the choices it requires, and the process that helps us forgive freely.

I'm grateful to realize that the better I understand forgiveness, the better I know the Father—the God who embodies forgiveness. And the opposite is just as true: the better I understand God, His nature and character, the better I learn to forgive. As a forgiveness apprentice, I have come to realize that forgiveness is the very heartbeat of God. Psalm 103 is a wonderful description of that heartbeat.

> Bless the LORD, O my soul,
> And forget none of His benefits;
> Who pardons all your iniquities. . . .
>
> The LORD is compassionate and gracious,
> Slow to anger and abounding in lovingkindness.
> He will not always strive with us,
> Nor will He keep His anger forever.
> He has not dealt with us according to our sins,
> Nor rewarded us according to our iniquities. (Ps.
>   103:2–3, 8–10)

I love the word *abounding* in verse 8! God's lovingkindness is overflowing, teeming, plentiful, bountiful. It knows no limits. The psalmist goes on, and the images he uses for the completeness of God's forgiveness are among my favorites:

> For as high as the heavens are above the earth,
> So great is His lovingkindness toward those who fear
>   Him.
> As far as the east is from the west,
> So far has He removed our transgressions from us.
> Just as a father has compassion on his children,
> So the LORD has compassion on those who fear Him.
>   (vv. 11–13)

What foundational truths do we learn of God's forgiveness in these verses? We learn *what motivates God's forgiveness*: God's abounding love. Pure and simple, God's reason for not treating us according to our sin is that He loves us so much, beyond measure. He wants nothing to stand in the way between us and Him.

We also learn *what God's forgiveness does*: it removes our iniquities (our sin and wrongdoing) from us completely. It actually separates us from the wrongs we have done so that God can relate to us on the basis of His love for us rather than on the basis of our sin.

There is a powerful word in verse 3 that describes this separation of us from our sin—*pardons*, which means that the offender is not required to pay any penalty for his or her wrongdoing. (Note that there is a difference between paying a penalty—a punishment—and suffering the natural consequences of our wrongful actions.)

Through these verses and so many others like them we see that God is all about forgiveness. It is His nature. It is His habit. Let's make it our habit as well! Do you want to live so near to the heart of God that you hear His heartbeat daily? Do you want your heart to beat as one with His? Then enter into the practice of forgiveness.

Theoretically that sounds great, doesn't it? Until we think about the person who has wounded us most deeply.

Must We Forgive?

What, then, of our forgiveness of others? After all, God is God. He is perfect and omnipotent, capable of anything. We are imperfect and limited in power. Just because God forgives, does that really mean we must forgive others? Why?

First, forgiveness is so important to God that He commands us to forgive. It is not a recommendation or a suggestion but a direct command. We already discussed in chapter 2 how Peter asked Jesus how many times we have to forgive someone and Jesus answered, "I do not say to you, up to seven times, but up to seventy times seven" (Matt. 18:22).

Just in case there are still any doubts in our minds about the command to forgive, consider this: When Jesus taught His disciples to pray in Matthew 6, He said, "'And forgive us our debts, as we also have forgiven our debtors.' . . . For if you forgive others for their transgressions, your heavenly Father will also forgive you. But if you do not forgive others, then your Father will not forgive your transgressions" (vv. 12, 14–15). Again, in Mark 11:25, Jesus instructs His disciples, "Whenever you stand praying, forgive, if you have anything against anyone, so that your Father who is in heaven will also forgive you your transgressions." Those are challenging verses, aren't they? Not only is the command to forgive others crystal clear but Jesus links our forgiveness of others to God's forgiveness of us. What does that mean?

I've read some who use that text to motivate us to forgive others out of fear that God will "get" us if we don't. I don't think that's what Jesus is saying in these passages. I believe that Jesus includes this startling warning to emphasize how serious God is about the importance of forgiving one another. Just like His statement, "If your eye causes you to stumble, pluck it out and throw it from you" (Matt. 18:9) wasn't literal but was said for shock value to make His point, perhaps the statement "But if you do not forgive others, then your Father will not forgive your transgressions" (6:15) is also not literal but is a radical statement to show how very serious His command to forgive really is.

If we consider the reasons and process for forgiveness yet are still *unwilling* to make the choice to forgive, then aren't we saying the cross was not enough? That is serious. That is a rejection of Jesus's redemptive work in our lives. That is acting as if our "wounding" is bigger than Jesus's wounds, that we have a right to hold on to unforgiveness. It reveals a lack of true understanding of the depth of our sin and the depth of Jesus's forgiveness. Any time we see God as less than He is and Christ's work as not sufficient for us, we are in perilous territory.

There are consequences to my unforgiveness (we'll be discussing them) just as there are consequences to my sin, and God does not want me to suffer either of those consequences. He is not saying here that we *earn* God's forgiveness by forgiving others (His forgiveness is given to us freely because of the sacrifice of His Son) but that the *refusal* to forgive others indicates that we have not yet surrendered ourselves fully to His lordship. After all, Jesus's entire purpose for His sacrifice was for our sins to be forgiven! Consider His words during the sacred moments of the Last Supper in Matthew 26:27–28: "Drink from it, all of you; for this is My blood of the covenant, which is poured out for many for forgiveness of sins." Forgiveness of sins was the reason He came to earth and was crucified. Obviously, He wants us to show the same grace and mercy to others as He has shown to us. He wants us to seek forgiveness when we've done wrong and to grant forgiveness freely.

To refuse to forgive is to have a bitter spirit. A bitter spirit puts a barrier between us and God (and usually others as well). Paul Thigpen writes, "Bitterness damages our relationship with God and blocks our experience of His forgiveness. What we refuse to grant to others, we reject for ourselves."[1] It doesn't mean we are going to hell but that our fellowship with God is broken. As a believer, we do not want to be in that position. It gives the enemy ground in our life and makes us vulnerable to the enemy's attacks.

The radical nature of Jesus's statement gets our attention and speaks to those who willfully, stubbornly choose not to forgive. If we truly have known the horror of our sin, the sting of our repentance, and the freedom of our forgiveness, then we will toss aside any stubborn refusal on our part and seek God's active help in forgiving.

Ephesians 4:32 sheds more light as it emphasizes that the command to forgive is the command to follow the example that Jesus has set for us: "Be kind to one another, tenderhearted, forgiving each other, just as God in Christ also has forgiven you." As an apprentice of forgiveness, I am inspired by this verse to overcome whatever resistance I have to forgiving another.

So, we've established that one reason we should strive to forgive others is that forgiveness is God's habit and heartbeat. Another reason is out of obedience to Jesus. Those are reasons enough! But while they are true and sound so spiritually strong and wise, we'd better deal honestly with this reality: forgiving others when they've wronged us is often difficult and sometimes seems downright impossible even if we *intend* to forgive. Let's confess that we all have internal resistance to forgiving those who have wronged us or wronged the ones whom we love.

I find there are some widely held misconceptions of forgiveness that not only feed that internal resistance but also keep many people secretly hiding the unforgiveness they carry, unable to or unwilling to move forward in obedience to God's command to forgive. It is far better to expose those misconceptions and deal with them rather than hide or ignore the unforgiveness that is lurking in our hearts. With that in mind, let's examine what forgiveness is not.

What Forgiveness Is Not

Forgiveness Is Not Natural

It is not human nature to automatically forgive a wrong. When wronged, we desire justice or even revenge. We are incensed and believe we deserve fairness. Our natural response is to be hurt or angered. We want offenders to humble themselves and seek our mercy, and we want to decide for ourselves if we will grant mercy and pardon or expect some price to be paid. To think, feel, and behave differently from all of those natural responses requires a supernatural change within us—the same supernatural force that was at work on the cross. Forgiveness is from God and is *super*natural.

Forgiveness Is Not Easy

Many people suspect that forgiveness comes easily to those who love the Lord, so they are ashamed that they struggle with it. Therefore, they hide or ignore their unforgiveness.

No, forgiveness does not come easily. I've spent far too many years listening to the whispered confessions and pain of those who attend my conferences to believe that, and the reading of many books and my own personal experiences confirm that forgiving others who have wronged us can be a great struggle, even for the spiritually mature.

How does a father or mother forgive the man who raped and murdered his or her daughter? How does a young wife forgive the husband who physically abused her? How does a man forgive his best friend for cheating with his wife? How does a survivor of sexual abuse forgive the priest or camp counselor or trusted coach or parent for molesting him or her as a child? How does a teenager forgive her parents for a dysfunctional and unsafe upbringing dominated by addiction, with its drug and alcohol abuse? How does a parent forgive a teenage son for stealing from him or her to buy drugs? How does a businessperson forgive a partner who swindled their profits away, leaving them in bankruptcy? How does a congregation forgive a pastor for stealing from the church funds or sexually harassing his or her young administrative assistant? How was I to forgive my first husband for years of infidelity while I was working hard to build a stronger marriage?

What about you? Do you find yourself straining at the mere thought of forgiving someone or some group of people? Perhaps you can empathize with the person who asks the questions, How can I forgive the terrorists who blew up my security and safety? How can I forgive her for betraying me when my eyes are red and swollen from tears? When I have screamed until my throat is dry? How do I forgive when I see the hole I pounded into my wall in a fit of rage? Or the bruises I try to cleverly disguise?

Forgiveness is raw. It's messy. But so is life—real life. At least in my experience. I have struggled with unfairness. I have struggled with my emotions—hurt, anger, hate, revenge. They came rolling in uninvited, wave after wave. I have struggled with how to be rid of them. They were not comfortable feelings. I have struggled with my thoughts. I know what it is to imagine all sorts of bad things happening to the person who hurt me. I've won every imaginary conversation as I rehearsed the confrontations I wanted to have with those who wounded me. But in the end, it didn't change anything. I was right back where I started—wrestling with unforgiveness.

We could fill pages with scenarios where forgiving another seems to expect more out of us than we are capable of giving. Let's agree. Forgiveness is a struggle, but it is worth the effort.

Forgiveness Is Not an Emotion

I think a lot of us assume that forgiveness is all about emotions, but it is not defined by how we feel. Yes, our emotions get involved, but forgiveness is a choice, an act of the will, a decision that, once made, becomes a process that is practiced. In that way it's a lot like love—not the emotional high of the sentiment of love, but the decision to commit yourself to the best interests of another no matter what comes and then acting on that decision. Too often when we feel negative emotions we assume that means we haven't yet forgiven. But emotions are not trustworthy. They shift and change for a vast variety of reasons. Emotions are not right or wrong, they just are. It's what we do with them—it is the choices that we make in light of our emotions—that demonstrate our forgiveness. We will discuss this further in chapter 6.

One day I was speaking to a young wife. "Ruth," she said, "some days I don't feel that I love my husband at all."

"I understand," I said, "but you made a vow, a commitment. Trust and act on that, not your shifting feelings." It is the same with the decision to forgive. I chose to forgive my first husband for his infidelity, but the emotions connected to betrayal and heartbreak took time (that felt like forever) and a lot of hard work to process through. It took counseling. I had to realize that I allowed mental conversations and thoughts to get me worked up emotionally, but we can't allow ourselves the luxury of such conversations. Beating up on somebody in our minds, stirring and fueling those negative emotions, is destructive. If we make the choice to forgive, eventually a tempering of emotions will likely follow the decision. You can forgive without emotion. Forgiveness is all about God—who He is and what He has done on the cross—rather than about our feelings.

Forgiveness Is Not Forgetting

Forgiveness actually involves remembering, not forgetting. In order for us to do the work of forgiving we must be able and willing to examine the situation, discern and tell ourselves the truth about it, and make the choice to forgive it. Trying to simply forget a painful situation is entering the unhealthy territory of repressing memories. Trying to forget can also be a lazy way to avoid forgiving, but that is avoidance, not genuine forgetting.

I suspect that the misconception that forgiving means we must forget comes from an erroneous interpretation of Isaiah 43:25, where God says, "I, even I, am the one who wipes out your transgressions for My own sake, and I will not remember your sins." That verse is saying that when we sin *it is God who chooses to forget our sin*. God is capable of choosing to forget, but unless I'm missing something, humans are not able to force themselves to forget. In fact, the harder we try to forget, the more likely we are to remember! Sadly, it seems the more painful the situation, the sharper our memory can be. I believe it would be a wonderful thing to forget, over time, the specifics of a wrong done to me once I've forgiven (after all, I sometimes forget in a minute why I just walked into a room!) but I leave that in God's hands since the recall capacity of the human brain is above my pay grade.

I am beholden to Dr. Lewis B. Smedes and his classic book *Forgive & Forget* for helping to shape my thinking on this subject of forgetting and remembering. He writes, "Forgetting, in fact, may be a dangerous way to escape the inner surgery of the heart that we call forgiving. There are two kinds of pain that we forget. We forget hurts too trivial to bother about. We forget pains too horrible for our memory to manage."[2] Then he goes on to say, "Once we have forgiven, however, we get a new freedom to forget. This time forgetting is a sign of health; it is not a trick to avoid spiritual surgery. We can forget because we have been healed."[3] Forgiving is remembering with the purpose of pardoning.

Forgiveness Is Not Dependent on the Offender's Actions or Attitudes

Remember that in forgiving we are following the example of Jesus, who, while hanging on the cross, called out,

"Father, forgive them; for they do not know what they are doing" (Luke 23:34). Those who were crucifying Him were not repentant. And remember Romans 5:8, "But God demonstrates His own love toward us, in that while we were yet sinners, Christ died for us." God's forgiveness is not dependent on our good behavior. Following God's example, we can forgive someone even if they have not changed their ways, even if they have not confessed, even if they have not asked for forgiveness or are flaunting their wrong. Forgiveness is about a decision we make, not that the offender makes.

And this point leads us into the next critically important distinction, the misunderstanding of which leads so many down the path of unforgiveness.

Forgiveness Is Not the Same as Reconciliation

Forgiveness means pardoning your offender and asking nothing as a prerequisite and nothing in return. It is freely given and literally requires nothing of the offender. Does that mean I am supposed to move on as if nothing happened? Does it mean wiping the slate clean? Putting on a happy face? Trusting and making myself vulnerable to the offender once again? No! Not necessarily.

Forgiveness is unconditional. Reconciliation, on the other hand, *is* conditional. Think of forgiveness as a one-way street from God to you to the offender, while reconciliation, as Dr. David Stoop says, "is a two-way street."[4] It requires agreement and efforts between two parties. There are times reconciliation would not be wise and would even cause greater harm. I heard my friend Dr. Ed Gungor say that there are some toxic people we have forgiven but need to keep a healthy distance from. We can go to the zoo and enjoy the animals, but we don't have to get in the cage with them! Sometimes it is healthier to remove yourself from a person or situation that is unhealthy. I made the comment above that I forgave my husband for his infidelities, and I did. Sadly, however, after efforts over several years to reconcile, I believed we were unable to continue as husband and wife, and we divorced after twenty-one years of marriage. Reconciliation is a complex subject addressed in more detail in chapter 6. But this we can say here: forgiveness is but one prerequisite for authentic reconciliation.

Let's review the common misconceptions above and consider how many have diverted us from the path of forgiveness. Then we'll take a moment to reinforce the last statement under each of the headings above. This provides a helpful summary of the truth about forgiveness.

- Forgiveness is from God and is *super*natural.
- Forgiveness is a struggle, but it is worth the effort.
- Forgiveness is all about God—who He is and what He has done on the cross—rather than about our feelings.
- Forgiving is remembering with the purpose of pardoning.
- Forgiveness is about a decision we make, not that the offender makes.
- Forgiveness is but one prerequisite for authentic reconciliation.

These corrections to our misguided thinking can go a long way in paving our pathway to commit ourselves to the high calling to live a life of forgiveness.

Forgiveness Is a Process

There is one more critically important aspect of forgiveness that we must address as we move forward, and that is this: *forgiveness is a process.* You will find the word *process* used many times throughout this book. I use it ten times in this chapter alone. Just as an apprentice binds him- or herself to a master over a period of time in order to learn a craft, so too forgiveness is a skill that must be practiced and refined over time. If we don't understand this, how easily we will feel defeated! If you take a look at the "forgiveness is" statements above, you will discover that we've discussed forgiveness in terms of our minds, our feelings, and our will. Meaningful change in any one of these three areas takes time and dedicated effort, but forgiveness requires internal change in each of these three aspects of our being.

Fortunately, the very first "forgiveness is" statement assures us that we are not alone in this process: forgiveness is *super*natural. This book is not a "self-help" book on how to work our way toward forgiving; it is a "God-help" book on recognizing God's desire to work forgiveness within us and opening ourselves to working with God on that effort. Can God supernaturally instill forgiveness in us in an instant? Yes; God is God and can accomplish anything He wills, including instant change in us. In my experience, however, and in the experience of most I have talked with, forgiveness is far more often a process than an instant change. We will be unpacking that process as we move forward, but expect that the changes that come with forgiveness will take time.

Years ago, when I began my wrestling match with forgiveness, I had no idea of the spiritual surgery God was about to begin on me. His scalpel has cut deep, rooting out decay and unhealthy attitudes, and the painful procedure has left me a changed woman, far healthier than I'd imagined. That surgery launched my ongoing apprenticeship in forgiveness.

I often say, "You can't steer a parked car." I think it's important that we are moving, and when we're moving in the right direction—closer to the heart of God—we can have confidence that God is reaching out toward us, drawing us further in. Beginning to understand the misconceptions we have about forgiveness is a wonderful place for us to start. However, understanding a few basics about what forgiveness *is* and *is not* leads us to an even bigger question: Do we really *want* to forgive, and if so, *why?* If it's going to take hard work and time, what is our personal motivation to forgive? Yes, we've established that God commands we forgive, but what is it that drives us to obey? My answer to that question has revolutionized the nature of my relationship with God, with my family, and with others. Are you ready to try to answer it for yourself?

FOUR

The Essence of Forgiveness

To forgive is much more than my emotional well-being.
It is an opportunity to enter into a divine grace and
sacred act.

Calvin Miller

A few years ago, my sweet friends James and Betty Robison, cohosts of TV's *Life Today*, sent me Sheila Walsh's book *The Longing in Me*. I read it immediately and absolutely loved it. There was, however, one part that left me in tears and pain as it exposed a wound—one that I'd buried long ago.

Sheila wrote that during a painful time in her life she was invited to visit my mother at her home in Montreat, North Carolina. She described sitting with Mother on the front porch in rocking chairs, enjoying the beautiful mountain view and talking. Effortlessly I imagined the scene in my

55

mind. It was a place so familiar to me—my childhood home nestled in the Blue Ridge Mountains.

Sheila was tired, so soon Mother showed her to the guest room upstairs. Sheila described the big, antique bed, freshly dressed in the lovely white linens Mother had bought in Switzerland. The room had a stunning view of the mountain range and the forested valley below. After tucking herself in, she heard a quiet knock on the door. Mother peeked around the door and asked if she could come in. She had a book in her hand.

Mother asked Sheila if she had ever read the old Scottish book *Beside the Bonnie Brier Bush* by Ian MacLaren. Sheila said she had not, so Mother asked if she'd mind if she read it to her.

I am sure Sheila was delighted as she read from the book. Mother was an excellent reader and was enchanting when she imitated the rich Scottish brogue as she did with us as children. Mother chose one of her very favorite stories in the book, "The Transformation of Lachlan Campbell," which has shades of the prodigal son story from the Gospel of Luke.

Sheila wrote, "I'll never forget that night or the grace that was lavished all over me by Ruth. As I left, she gave me her copy of the book."[1]

As I read Sheila's words, tears sprung to my eyes and I found myself weeping with grief. Weeks later, I realized, to my chagrin, I had not yet written Sheila a thank-you note. I sat down to write one before more time passed, knowing that I had to deal with the buried pain her book had surfaced within me.

In my note to Sheila I wrote, "I believe what delayed me in writing to you was your telling how my mother cared for you

. . . how she seemed to understand . . . her grace. It was painful to read because Mother had a difficult time doing that for me. I have come to understand her actions and I know she loved me, but in my pain I withdrew. I felt I had been a huge disappointment to her. I knew God loved broken people, but I didn't feel my mother liked having a broken daughter and certainly did not like me talking about my brokenness! It was okay for you, her guest, but not her daughter."

It was painful to me that my mother could be so understanding with others' failings but not, in my estimation, with me—her daughter. As I read Sheila's story I was surprised by the thoughts, emotions, and pain that came over me. I thought I had dealt with it all years before. But forgiveness, as we have discussed, is a process that takes time.

Sheila's experience with Mother was not the only one that caused those same feelings to surface. From my wounded perspective, it had often seemed easier for Mother to be with others than with me. There was a little street waif in London named Wendy. There was a drug addict from New York, Tony, who had been converted while in her Sunday school class. She loved that class and they loved her. Mother loved the young people who came to our home— many were Franklin's and Anne's friends they brought home from school. (I went away to boarding school.) She would sit up late discussing all manner of topics with them with openness and understanding. But I didn't have that same nature, so often I felt left out. I doubt she even knew it. The passage in Sheila's book had surfaced a deep longing for my mother and familiar old feelings of always being on the outside looking in, but never truly belonging. As I was the middle child of five, that seemed to be a sensitive spot for me. I could see I had some forgiveness work to do on this old buried wound.

Mother was gone by then, so there was no way to explore healing together. This wound would have to be dealt with just between God and me. And this is an important point in our discussion of forgiveness. No matter what the wound or wrong, no matter who may or may not be involved in bringing the matter to the point of forgiveness and resolution, we have the opportunity to *begin* the forgiveness process with the one Person who is central to our experience of forgiveness: Jesus.

Some time ago, I heard or read somewhere a concept that was fresh to me. It has deepened my understanding of forgiveness. *Forgiveness is a way to make our wounds sacred.*

Making Our Wounds Sacred

A wound by its very nature is ugly and unpleasant. For a moment, just think about an unkind remark made to you or the feelings that stirred within you when you were betrayed or rejected or wronged. Something happens in our spirit—it is wounded, our heart is bruised, an internal alarm goes off to let us know we are stung deeply.

What is our first response to a wound? We react. We may grimace and recoil, we may cry out in pain or fear or panic. We may strike out in retaliation or anger or vengeance, or we may cower, retreat, or withdraw. But whatever our initial instinctual reaction, one thing is certain: once we are wronged or wounded by another, we have a choice as to what we do with that wound. We can seek healing for it, or we can leave it to fester.

The choice to heal often means the painful cleansing and binding up of our wounds. On the other hand, the choice of leaving wounds untended guarantees they will fester and become infected, which does more damage in the long run. Obviously, when we put it that way, it's clear what the better choice is: choose healing. But when it comes to deep wounds in relationships, the two pathways—healing versus festering—can create an internal dilemma. Why? Because either way there is pain to be endured, and sometimes it's tempting to let it slide, to let it fester, rather than take the painful proactive steps involved in cleaning and binding up a wound.

For example, my "mother wound," like many relationship wounds, was complicated. Did Mother wrong me by showering her attention and nurture on Sheila or my sisters or brothers or others in her life? No. Those weren't wrongs she committed against me—they were lovely examples of her giving her best to others. Yet, as I observed from "the outside looking in," my own quiet and reserved middle-child issues festering, I felt wounded. It seemed Mother didn't do the same for me as she did for others. I felt terribly guilty for feeling that way about my precious mother, but emotions don't usually listen to reason. (Looking back, I know she tried, but the dynamics between us were so different that her way of loving me took on a different shape. It always seemed awkward between us.)

I had two wounds that needed to be addressed. One, I needed to forgive Mother for not nurturing me in the way I could receive it. Two, I had to recognize the jealousy and resentment on my part for the type of care she gave others. I needed to seek God's forgiveness and then learn to forgive myself. But for years, though I longed to be free of those two issues, I couldn't find the path to healing. Those wounds got buried deep and contributed to feelings of being inadequate. They also left me feeling guilty of ingratitude.

Let's pause for a moment and step into thinking about this new concept of making our wounds sacred. To make something sacred is to dedicate it to God for His use, to elevate something to the status of *holy*—reflecting the character and nature of God.

How would we do that? What would happen if, when we are wounded, we were to "make it sacred" by dedicating it to God? *Lord, here is my open, painful wound. I give it to You to use as You see fit. Please use it, Lord, to accomplish something good. Take it and transform it from an ugly wound to an example of Your transforming power and holy character.*

Let's take my two wounds—longing for mother love and jealous resentment—and see what they look like when I offer them to God so they can be transformed into examples of God's holy character and nature in me. Through some work on my part, I tried to look at these wounds through new eyes—eyes searching for evidence of God's character and nature at work. And, sure enough, I found that evidence!

Through the years, God gave me some wonderful surrogates who helped satisfy my longing of closeness with a mother. My sister Anne was one shining example. All through my growing up years, Anne and I were very close. Though only a few years older than me, she was a steady and reliable source of love and guidance. When I thought it was time for me to begin shaving my legs, I felt awkward going to my mother, so I asked Anne to go talk to Mother for me. I talked with Anne, not my mother, about my boyfriends.

Anne and I shared a love for horses and often rode together at a local stable. Then there was "Aunt" Mary Helen Wilson—not a real aunt, but someone who lived nearby and listened well. She only had two children but enough mothering in her for twelve. After my first child was born, Martha Ayers, a lovely lady in the Philadelphia area, mentored me. By recognizing the role of these other godly women in my life, I could see God's provision of my longed-for mother love. I was nurtured. I was included in their lives. Through them, God saw to it that mother love was lavished upon me in a language I could understand.

While searching for evidence of God's nature and character at work, I looked back with gratitude that it was Mother who encouraged me to write. On my thirteenth birthday she gave me a green leather journal for my writing. (My habit of journaling started then and continues to this day.) When I suggested she revise the 1820s children's Bible storybook *First Steps for Little Feet along Gospel Paths*, a book we had used as children that was by then very out-of-date, she turned to me and suggested I do the rewrite. I did! And the result was a lovely Bible storybook, *Step into the Bible*. When I was away at boarding school, Mother was faithful every week to write me letters of news from home, giving this very homesick daughter advice she'd learned during her own years away from her home while at boarding school in North Korea.

I chuckled as I thought of the time I visited my parents in St. Martin. I became quite ill and needed to be airlifted back to the United States for medical treatment, but the small airport was closed for the night; I had to wait until the next morning. Mother was worried. She came into my room to give me a back rub even though all she had for lotion was anti-wrinkle cream! What an endearing example of mother love.

In giving my wound to God, I realized my wonderful memories of Mother and so wrote a book about her, *Legacy of Love*. She was truly a remarkable lady. Later, in my book *Fear Not Tomorrow, God Is Already There*, I told of her death. I was concerned at the time that my heart had been closed off and shuttered by hurts and misunderstandings. I asked God to let me know I loved her. As I tended her body in the quiet while others were out calling other family members, an overwhelming love for her filled me and comforted me.

All these memories demonstrated that God had been gracious in giving me such a godly and wise mother, and He had already done much healing work in me. In the process, my wounds were replaced with a forgiving and grace-filled spirit.

Making our wounds sacred has the power to transform them. In the giving of our wounds over to God for His service, we are saying, *Lord, yes, this hurts. But I'm giving it to You for Your use. Transform it into something that reflects You and Your relentless love. Give it a holy purpose I can see and recognize.* When we dedicate our wounds to God, we know that He won't waste them but will use them for His glory and our good. So then, let's keep our eyes open for the evidence of God's grace and work in the midst of our pain. This will begin to replace the pain with anticipation. Not immediately, but in time.

Making our wounds sacred—dedicating them to God and His service—is foundational to forgiveness as it invites God to transform our wounds into spiritual strengths instead of black holes of despair and resentment. This provides a springboard to Christlike love and grace—the ultimate antidote to a lack of forgiveness.

My friend Amy discovered the power of making our wounds sacred as she dealt with her young adult son who was a drug addict. Over a period of years, she'd tried in many ways to respond with love and support through her son's on-again, off-again drug abuse. When he was abusing drugs, he'd often lose his job. She helped him time and again to pay his rent or his car insurance or get into rehab programs. Then, when he'd come clean and was able to work, she'd invite him to live in her home while he got on his feet. But just as she'd think he was on track, he'd lie and steal her cash or belongings to go buy drugs, and she'd have to insist he leave her home. The cycle went on for years: lying, stealing, and deception interspersed with regrets, begging forgiveness, efforts toward recovery, and responsible choices, then right back to drugs again.

Over time, Amy recognized that her wounds of anger, resentment, and bitterness toward her son were at war with her compassion and desire to help him. She knew she couldn't control her son's choices, but what was she to do with the emotional and spiritual wounds she was carrying? She couldn't allow her son's dysfunction to cripple her own emotional and spiritual health. She wanted to forgive her son but not enable him. She needed healing for her wounds in the midst of her son's dysfunction, regardless of the life choices he was making.

By making her wounds sacred—dedicating them to God for His use and glory no matter how painful or ugly they were— she began a pathway toward healing and forgiveness. God honored Amy's request, like mine, that He use her wounds for His use, and in the process Amy experienced the next foundation of forgiveness that we are going to explore.

Displaying the Character of God

"How, Lord," Amy had to ask, "can you take my anger and bitterness toward my son and use them for your purposes?" Romans 12:2 gave her a clue: "And do not be conformed to this world, but be transformed by the renewing of your mind, so that you may prove what the will of God is, that which is good and acceptable and perfect."

This verse gave her hope. God could transform her anger and bitterness into something good and acceptable.

Like the concept we discussed above, this would take some spiritual work on her part. She had to begin by being transparent and honest with God, and that meant recognizing the sin beneath her wounds. She had to tell herself the truth. She wrote to me,

> *I had to realize that my love for my son was tainted with selfishness and sin. Pure love would not expect or ask for anything in return, but I was angry and bitter because I expected good behavior on his part. My love for him wasn't as unconditional as I liked to think. His bad behavior resulted in me wanting to strike out and retaliate. I wanted him to pay.*

Amy began the process of forgiving her son by confessing to God her own selfishness and sin and asking Him to transform her love into unconditional love, the kind of love described in 1 Corinthians 13. She zeroed in on verse 5, asking for a love that "does not act unbecomingly; it does not seek its own, is not provoked, does not take into account a wrong suffered." This prayer resulted in her beginning to anticipate how God would change her rather than how her son would change. She had made her wounds sacred!

Now for her new discovery. Amy's new understanding of God using her wounds of bitterness and anger as tools in His hands to demonstrate His holy character led her to see her relationship with her son as a parable of sorts—a representation of God's relationship to His wayward people, a microcosm of God's love for her.

If I, in all of my sinfulness and selfishness, could still love my son no matter what life choices he made, how much more must God love me? My understanding of my love for my son was transformed. In loving him, I saw that I was modeling God's love for His people, for me, for my son. I was actually displaying the character of God. It became easier to exercise tough love and allow him to suffer his own consequences without stepping in to rescue him.

I searched the Scriptures and saw how many times God allowed His wayward people to suffer the consequences for their actions, yet still love them, still send His Word through the prophets, still stand ready to be their deliverer when they would turn back to Him and His ways. When my son became homeless in the midst of his drug abuse, I was able to love yet not rescue. He called me one night, cold and hungry, and I was able to say without anger or bitterness, "I'm sorry you are hurting. I'm sad that you keep choosing drugs over self-care. Do you know how to get to the nearest homeless shelter? Good then. I hope you choose to go there." I hung up grieving for him, but not angry at him. My anger and bitterness began to melt away while my love remained vibrant and steadfast.

Amy's wounds of bitterness and anger were healing even when her son did not change his ways. His drug abuse continued, yet Amy found herself free to love her son without rescuing him. Eventually, he wound up in prison. Here, her love could continue to express itself in visits and letters and in accepting phone calls during which she could express her love and concern. And when his prison sentence was over, she was able to be instrumental in arranging a Christian home that could serve as his "halfway house" as he found a job and plugged into a drug recovery program. Today, years later, her son is drug free, self-sufficient, and responsible. For that she is grateful. She knows how blessed they are that he survived and eventually flourished. But she also knows that any day he may slip back into addiction. Notably, her relationship with her son is still solid and loving without the baggage of any residual anger and bitterness.

There is something critically important in Amy's story that I don't want you to miss. She wrote, "I saw that I was modeling God's love for His people, for me, for my son."

Yes! The concept we all need to grasp when it comes to forgiveness is this: *when we forgive, we are displaying the character of God.*

I am not saying that it is easy. Forgiveness goes against our nature. We strain against it. We argue. We fight for our rights. We nurse our hurts. We walk in self-pity and carry bitterness. But in the end, we come down to this very simple truth: Jesus said to forgive over and over and over and over again. Forgiveness reflects His nature. That's what He did *for* us. That's what He wants *from* us. That is what He is doing *in* us. And isn't that what we ultimately want?

Forgiveness is a sacred sacrifice you offer to God, a gift you give to Him. It is an opportunity to practice a divine quality. Let's elevate forgiveness to the realm of the holy. It's about having the opportunity to model and display God's character to a broken world in desperate need of true forgiveness.

This perspective not only provides a great motivator to forgive but taps into the ultimate purpose of God's people showing forgiveness—to glorify God and make Him known to others. Doing so means saying, "I'm going to make my decisions not based on what I want, such as validation or revenge, and not based on what I feel, such as anger and bitterness, but based instead on my purpose, which is to glorify God." I cannot think of a more powerful way to make our wounds sacred than making ourselves available to display the character of God.

Participating in a Miracle

We've transformed our approach to forgiveness by making our wounds sacred. We've elevated forgiveness to the realm of the holy by understanding that forgiveness is displaying the character of God. Now let's experience forgiveness by participating in a miracle.

I love how Webster's Dictionary defines a miracle: "an extraordinary event manifesting divine intervention in human affairs."[2] Yes! Exactly. Forgiveness is certainly an extraordinary event displaying God's intervention in human affairs. It is God who has modeled for us what forgiveness looks like. If we choose to show mercy when wronged, we are tapping into God's mercy. If we choose to pardon the offender, we are imitating God's pardon of us. Prior to Jesus's crucifixion, God required a blood sacrifice before He granted forgiveness. He sent Jesus to earth as the one blood sacrifice to atone for all our sin—the ultimate divine intervention in human affairs! Miraculously, then, you and I are forgiven for our sins while we are yet sinners.

What fascinates me about forgiveness is that through it God invites us to participate with Him in this miracle. We have a part to play and choices to make—when we submit our wounds for transformation to His holy use and choose to display His character to the world, God will "intervene in our affairs" and actually change our hearts from bitterness to love, from resentment to restoration. This is miraculous.

Amy experienced miraculous intervention in her life through forgiveness when God transformed her anger and bitterness against her son into compassionate love with no strings attached. She came to a point where she was able to embrace him with absolutely no resentment whether he was high on drugs, homeless, in prison, or hospitalized or was clean and sober, in rehab, and living responsibly. "The difference in my heart toward my son is nothing short of a miracle," she told me.

I have experienced God's miraculous intervention in my life through forgiveness in so many ways. Years ago, when I was reeling in pain from sin—my husband's, others', and my own—I wept as I told God, "If You can ever use this mess, You are welcome to it!" I dedicated my ugly, painful wounds to Him to use for His purpose, never imagining how He could actually use them. I was prepared to hide away for the rest of my life—so full of shame and guilt. But I had heard countless stories of lives transformed by His grace, so I knew He could work a miracle. I wanted Him to do so in my messy life. And He did. God answered that prayer by inspiring me to write *In Every Pew Sits a Broken Heart*, which has ministered to thousands. God literally transformed my pain into something that He used for His kingdom and uses still.

How does a woman go from planning to slit her wrists in despair to leading Ruth Graham & Friends into prisons? Only by a miracle.

When I stood outside Michael's cell in Angola Prison and listened to this brutal murderer sing "It Is Well with My Soul," and then heard from the murdered boy's grandfather that he'd been praying for Michael's salvation, I knew beyond a doubt I was witnessing the miraculous.

Forgiveness is an invitation to the miraculous! And *you* can experience divine intervention in *your* affairs. I pray that you will. I pray that you will begin in the three specific ways we've discussed in this chapter.

Choose to make your wounds sacred.

Choose to display the character of God.

Choose to participate in the miraculous.

FIVE

The Power of Grace

Like a sudden thaw in the middle of winter, grace happens at unexpected moments. It stops us short, catches our breath, disarms. If we manipulate it, try to control it, somehow earn it, that would not be grace.

Philip Yancey

If we are to grasp a fresh understanding of forgiveness that is powerful enough to penetrate our pain, bitterness, and shame, we must explore grace. *Grace* to many of us is one of those "religious" words that may seem rather vague and mysterious. For many years I thought I understood its meaning. Many Bible dictionaries and resources define it as "the unmerited favor of God." *Unmerited* means undeserved, not earned. *Grace*, as defined in my Bible dictionary, includes, "that which brings delight, joy, happiness, or good fortune."[1] Words like *favor*, *kindness*, *generosity*, and *mercy* are often used to define grace. Theologically, I got the message: we

71

don't deserve God's love and we haven't earned it, but He loves us anyway. And yes, that is correct.

But a "correct" understanding and a "heartfelt" understanding can be two different things. There was one pivotal moment in my life when my awareness of the depth and fullness of grace became quite real and personal. This moment above all others ushered in a transforming understanding of forgiveness. I've told this story many times. I wrote about it in *In Every Pew Sits a Broken Heart*. I even told it at my father's funeral, so bear with me if you've heard it before, for I want us to explore how this grace-filled moment became a foundation of my ability to forgive myself and forgive others.

Welcome Home

After my pain-filled divorce from my first husband of twenty-one years and my subsequent depression, my family recommended that I move to get a fresh start in new surroundings. I chose to move near my oldest sister, Gigi. I'd enjoy her company and I knew there was a good church nearby. So I packed up my life and my three children and moved from the beautiful, rural Shenandoah Valley of Virginia to the downtown of a large city in Florida. My children were very unhappy with the move. They'd grown up on a farm, and this new environment was foreign to them. In theory, the move seemed like a good idea to me, but in reality, I was a fish out of water.

It wasn't long before my new pastor introduced me to a handsome widower, and we began to date fast and furiously. My children didn't like him, but I figured they were almost grown. I told myself I wasn't going to let them dictate my choices. My family was nervous over how fast I was moving. Mother called me from Seattle and Daddy called me from Tokyo; both cautioned me to slow down. But I reasoned that they'd never been divorced. They'd never been a single parent. What did they know? There were red flags, but I chose to ignore them. I turned to the Scriptures but manipulated them to fit my own desires and thinking. So, being stubborn, willful, and sinful, I rushed into marrying this man on New Year's Eve, only six months after meeting him.

Within twenty-four hours I knew I'd made a terrible mistake. After five weeks, I fled. I was afraid of him. I wanted to run away and hide from everyone. But I couldn't run. I couldn't hide. I had to confront my mistake and myself. I had to humble myself and ask for forgiveness from God, my children, my family, and myself. And the place to start was with my parents. I knew I had to go see them and talk to them.

Mother and Daddy were home in Montreat, so I called to let them know I was coming and made the two-day drive from Florida to North Carolina. As the miles passed, my doubts plagued me. How could I ever trust myself again? What would Mother and Daddy think of me? What would they say? That I had made my bed and now had to lie in it? That they were ashamed of me? I certainly was ashamed of myself. My fears multiplied with every mile. As I wound up the long mountain driveway to our home, fear had the upper hand. I was filled with shame and guilt. I saw myself as I was—sinful and in need of grace and mercy. I was desperate for forgiveness and love but felt totally undeserving of it. Adrenaline kept my foot on the gas as fear gripped the steering wheel.

As I rounded the last bend in my parents' driveway, I saw my father standing there, waiting for me. The time had come. I had to face Daddy. What would he say? There was no one in my life whose love and approval meant more to me. As I turned off the ignition, Daddy approached. I opened the car door and . . .

We must stop here and linger for just a moment, for this is the moment of truth. I braced for the unknown and my shame felt unbearable.

Daddy stepped toward me, spread his long arms wide, wrapped me in his tight embrace, and said to me in his rich, warm voice, "Welcome home."

I melted into that embrace, knowing in that instant that I was loved unconditionally. In Daddy's arms I was safe, both emotionally and physically. I was immersed in mercy. I was forgiven.

I was wrapped in grace. Unmerited. Undeserved. Merciful. Generous. Billy Graham was not God, but he modeled God's grace for me. Never again would the theological definition of the word *grace* be just an academic concept for me. It was now a personal experience. In the epigraph above, Philip Yancey captures the impact of grace perhaps better than I've ever seen: "Like a sudden thaw in the middle of winter. . . . It stops us short, catches our breath, disarms."[2] That's how I felt in Daddy's arms.

Recognizing Grace Lavished upon Us

Ephesians 1:7–8 says, "In Him we have redemption through His blood, the forgiveness of our trespasses, according to the riches of His grace which He lavished on us."

A foundation was laid for me in my parents' driveway that day. One that I could build upon. This experience gave me the courage to begin my baby steps in the process of forgiveness—both receiving it and, in response, giving it. And I do mean baby steps! Remember what I said in chapter 3: forgiveness is a process that takes time. Daddy's welcome home gave me a taste of God's grace. If God could forgive me, then I could learn to forgive myself. I could find the courage to ask the forgiveness of my children and family. Perhaps I'd even be able to reflect that grace enough to grow in forgiveness toward my ex-husband and others who had wounded me in the wake of the divorce. Lucinda Secrest McDowell writes she was "transformed by an encounter with Jesus who stooped and lifted me out of my pit, relocating me to holy ground."[3] That's what grace did for me. That's what it can do for you.

Search your memory for your own experiences of being given grace. You may have had a powerful experience directly with God, perhaps at the point of your conversion, or at a time when you came to God in a spirit of deep repentance. Have you ever come to the Lord heavy with the weight of your own sin and actually sensed that weight lifted from you? If so, meditate on that moment. Remember that relief. That was grace. Or maybe you, like me, were forgiven, accepted, or embraced by someone else when you didn't deserve it. Perhaps you've stood in a court of law, guilty, and were granted leniency. Maybe you'll need to think all the way back to your childhood, when you were let off the hook after some wrong you committed. Whatever your taste of grace, allow that experience to be your model for how God embraces you in spite of your unworthiness.

The Bible is a book full of grace stories. We know the grace revealed to the prodigal son when he returned to his father. We know the grace Jesus extended to the woman taken in adultery. We know the grace given the thief dying alongside Jesus. All were undeserving, yet all were offered the gift of grace. I believe that one reason God gives us so many grace stories is that He knows we need to be told over and over again. We need inspiration, models, and examples. He knows we have short memories and need reminders. He knows how hard it is for us to wrap our heads and hearts around the truth and power of this grace of His, for grace is "other" than us. It is foreign. It is God's nature, not our own. But it is so important that we understand and embrace God's grace. Why? Because if Almighty God says I am forgiven, who am I to argue? If God values me enough to lavish His grace on me, who am I to withhold forgiveness from myself?

Believing that God has lavished His grace upon us is Forgiveness 101. Everything else we learn about forgiveness is built on that foundation. Use your imagination to put yourself in the same kind of situation I was in as I drove to see my parents. Your sins are in the forefront of your thinking, and you are listing them one by one. Or maybe you are overwhelmed by one sin you cannot seem to defeat. Ashamed. Embarrassed. Guilty. Unable to make any more excuses. You brace yourself to face your Father God. Hesitantly, you look to Him. Instead of anger and disapproval, you see love and tenderness. You feel God's embrace and hear His "welcome home" for you. That is receiving grace.

Now to give grace. Ask yourself: If your "enemy," someone who has wounded you deeply, were to come to you, would you be able to wrap your arms around him or her with your own welcome home? Are you not there yet? Then let's move one step closer to that point.

Lavishing Grace on Those Who Have Wronged Us

Grace, once received, multiplies and flows back out of us if we allow it to. What will it take for you to extend your grace to those who wound you? Let's turn to a story Jesus told to His disciples, known as the Parable of the Unmerciful Servant, found in Matthew 18:21–35 (my paraphrase). A king wanted to settle accounts with his servants. A servant who owed him ten thousand bags of gold was brought before him. He wasn't able to pay, so the king ordered him, his wife, and his children sold to pay off the debt. But the servant fell on his knees before the king and begged for the king's patience, promising to pay back everything. The king showed mercy, canceled the debt completely, and let the man go. Grace.

The servant then encountered a man who owed him a hundred silver coins. He grabbed the man and began choking him, demanding the man pay what was due. This man fell to his knees and begged his fellow servant for patience, promising to pay it back, but he refused and had the man thrown into prison until he could pay the debt.

Now, the other servants witnessed all of this and were outraged, so they went to the king and told him everything that had happened. Let's read the rest directly from Matthew 18:32–35:

> Then summoning him, his lord said to him, "You wicked slave, I forgave you all that debt because you pleaded with me. Should you not also have had mercy on your fellow slave,

in the same way that I had mercy on you?" And his lord, moved with anger, handed him over to the torturers until he should repay all that was owed him. My heavenly Father will also do the same to you, if each of you does not forgive his brother from your heart.

Clearly, our heavenly Father, who demonstrated His abundant grace to us at Calvary, wants us, in return, to show grace to those who wrong us, whether it be someone in our family, a coworker, a boss, a friend, or someone in the church. Remember that we aren't alone in this process. God works in and through us as we make our wounds sacred, display His character, and participate in the miraculous. Forgiveness is the work God is doing—we need only to offer ourselves to be a channel of His grace. I suggest that if you are struggling to forgive someone else for his or her wrongs against you, it may be possible that you've not yet fully grasped the grace that has been given to you. Why? Do you suspect deep down that you are unworthy—that if your ugly behaviors and worst thoughts and feelings, hidden deep inside, were known, you would not be wrapped in God's welcome home embrace? Then let's take a look at a truc story.

An Unlikely Grace Story

In the book of Joshua, God introduces us to a woman who may have felt unworthy of God's embrace—who never dreamed she had a part to play in passing along God's grace to others. Her story paints another picture of the power of grace, though you may have never recognized it as such. As her story unfolds, watch for the evidence of God's embrace of her and how she, in turn, extended grace to others she could have considered enemies.

Rahab was a woman who lived in the large city of Jericho during the time Joshua took over leadership of the Israelites after Moses. Her life was probably lonely on many levels, though she was rarely alone. Her family didn't associate with her much. Picture her stone house at the far side of Jericho, in an area of the city where no one wanted to live. Only the poor and those with less-desirable occupations settled there. The rear of her house was built into the city wall, a vulnerable place to be in the event of an attack. Her home, and homes like hers, would be the first to encounter an enemy in war.

If she leaned out her window in this wall, she could see the gate at one end of the city and the rolling hills along the other.

Rahab kept her home ready at any moment for the "visitors" who often dropped by. The main entrance to most buildings in the city faced the street. But since her visitors had something to hide, the door to her home was on the side of the house rather than the front, giving less fodder for peering eyes and gossiping tongues. Her guests could slip inside without advertising to the rest of the city where they were.

Very soon after Moses died, God gave Joshua orders to cross the Jordan River ten miles west of their encampment and claim the land of promise given to Abraham. As a shrewd military leader, Joshua didn't just gather up a bunch of his buddies and tumble into the land without thought. He made a plan for the first step in the conquest of this great land. He secretly sent in spies to check out Jericho—a walled fortress of a city located about seven miles on the other side of the Jordan River from where they were encamped.

The spies were also shrewd. It's likely they dressed as travelers passing through the area who desired what traveling men often do—the pleasure of a woman's company with whom they could have a tryst without any obligation beyond payment for services rendered. The perfect cover to check out the city.

As the spies passed through the city gates, they looked for someone to approach, a man who might be able to direct them to a place of "lodging." They presumed the homes of prostitutes would be located with the poor at the far end of the city, as they usually were. This kept their undesirable behavior separate from the more upstanding, moral citizens. The ruse of looking for such female company allowed them to pass through the whole city, gaining intelligence and taking stock of all an army might need to know before they raided it.

Rahab warmly welcomed the men who appeared at the door of her little stone house on the top of the outer Jericho wall and invited them in, leading them to the rooftop where they could chat and perhaps negotiate a price. Having strange men come to her door looking for lodging wasn't unusual for her. She'd hosted many a traveler in her little house—men who came to share her bed and her body before continuing their journey. She didn't limit her services to travelers, however—she welcomed many men from throughout the city and surrounding villages, anyone who could pay.

It wasn't long before she discovered the men were not there for the usual reason. Just as they revealed themselves to her, she heard her name spoken by strong voices below;

two men were in the street, dressed in the garb of the king's loyal men. She peered over the side of the roof and saw a woman with a water pot on her head point in the direction of Rahab's house.

Rahab had ceased to be flustered by the unexpected long ago. Her quick mind set her to task, and after she hid the spies she moved down the ladder quickly. She arranged her clothing to what would be expected by a visitor to a home such as hers. When the king's men announced their presence at her door, she was able to meet them with a broom in one hand and the other placed on her hip, a jeweled ring (a gift from a patron) on her finger. "Yes," she said, dipping in a quick bow. "How may I help the messengers of the king?"

"Bring out the men who have come to you, who have entered your house, for they have come to search out all the land."

She had long ago learned to be quite skilled at becoming what a man wanted by creating a believable façade through changing her voice and altering her facial expressions to produce the illusion she needed. So, for these king's men, she took on a quizzical look that turned to surprise. "Yes, the men came to me, but I didn't know where they were from." She flashed the king's men a knowing smile. "After all, I do see many travelers, but we do not generally discuss where they are from or where they are going. We have a more immediate transaction to make."

The taller of the king's men cleared his throat, and the other, an older man who was not a stranger to Rahab, blushed.

"Step aside," the less affected man said. "We need to search your home."

She gave a slight bow, sweeping her arm to welcome them inside. It didn't take long for them to inspect the interior of the home and check out the roof, where they saw stalks of flax laid out in neat rows to dry. "You could teach my wife a thing or two," the older man said, then blushed again, hurrying to clarify what he meant. "She just throws the flax haphazardly about."

"When did they leave?" the taller man interrupted, ushering them outdoors once again.

"They wanted to leave before the gates closed, not wanting to spend the night." She leaned forward, conspiratorially. "I don't think they wanted to pay for that much of my time."

The older man shifted to an authoritative tone. "Do you know where they went?"

"No. But if you pursue them quickly, I'm sure you will overtake them," she said, pointing toward the city gates and beyond.

The king's men spun on their heels without thanking her or saying goodbye as they began their pursuit before the city gate was shut for the night. Rahab watched as the men gathered a handful of others and sped out through the gate. The moment they were through, the gates swung closed, followed by the dull tone of metal against metal as the bolts slid through their anchors.

Rahab greeted the few neighbors out for an evening's stroll, speaking intentionally about the heat and how she intended to spend the evening enjoying the cooler air from her roof.

Her playacting complete, she climbed the ladder to her roof, moved aside the stalks of flax to uncover the spies, and motioned for them to sit close.

"I know who you are," she said quietly. The pretense she had put on for the king's men vanished from her lips and her heart. Instead, she set her authentic heart before them. "I know the Lord has given you this land. We've heard the stories of how your God delivered you out of Egypt. How He dried up the waters of the Red Sea before you. We have heard how you utterly destroyed the two kings of Sihon and Og. Our hearts have melted. No courage has remained in any man. For the Lord your God, He is God in heaven above and on earth beneath" (see Josh. 2:9–11).

The men were astounded by her belief in God. It was the last thing they would have expected from a citizen in Jericho—especially from a harlot.

Her next words also display faith. "Now then, please swear to me by the Lord that you will show kindness to my family, because I have shown kindness to you. Give me a sure sign that you will spare the lives of my father and mother, my brothers and sisters, and all who belong to them—and that you will save us from death" (see vv. 12–13).

The spies marveled that not only did she believe God was going to send His army but that army was going to be successful at destroying her city.

"Our lives for your lives!" the men assured her. "If you don't tell what we are doing, we will treat you kindly and faithfully when the Lord gives us the land" (see v. 14). They advised her to place their scarlet cord in the window as a sign so their invading army would not harm those within that house.

After exchanging these vows and promises, Rahab gives them more life-saving advice. "Go to the hills so the pursuers will not find you. Hide yourselves there three days until they return, and then go on your way" (see v. 16).

Sometime in the dark of night, knowing she was risking her life in doing so, she lowered them through her window, down the wall of the city. The men did as she said, hiding in the hills for three days before taking their vital information back to Joshua. It wasn't long before the seven-day march around the walls of Jericho, with its shouts and trumpets, and the spies were soon racing in to fulfill their promise to Rahab, rescuing her and all who were there with her. She had shown them grace; now they extended grace to her.

The story of Rahab could have ended there. Certainly, there are plenty of stories of women who appear once in Scripture and that's the only time we hear of them. But in Rahab's case, after the story of her rescue is complete, we hear about her three more times in Scripture—all of them rather astounding. After all, who was Rahab? She was a nobody. A foreigner. She was not an Israelite. She was not one of God's chosen children, so how easy it is to assume she was outside the realm of faith and salvation. And talk about a sinner! The new commandments given the Israelites called for the death of a harlot like her. She lived a life of sin.

Yet God chose to send the spies to *her* door. Undeserved. Unearned. She recognized the opportunity to save her entire family, and so she extended grace to these strangers by risking her own life for them.

The first time we hear her name again is when Matthew is listing the lineage of Jesus (Matt. 1:5), which includes the names of just five women—almost lost in a sea of men's names—three of whom are known for their stories of shame, stories that one would think would exclude them from such a holy bloodline. Here we discover that Rahab is the great King David's great-great-grandmother!

Rahab also appears in Hebrews 11, the New Testament's list of the heroes of faith. "By faith the walls of Jericho fell down after they had been encircled for seven days. By faith Rahab the harlot did not perish along with those who were disobedient, after she had welcomed the spies in peace" (vv. 30–31). And then James 2:24–26 reads, "You see that a man is justified by works and not by faith alone. In the same way, was not Rahab the harlot also justified by works when she received the messengers and sent them out by another way? For just as the body without the spirit is dead, so also faith without works is dead."

So, what do we make of this story? In what ways did Rahab receive God's grace? Of all the people God could have chosen to interact with the spies, He chose her, though she was a harlot, to save their lives and, by so doing, provide the Israelites with the intelligence they needed to plan their attack.

Once she learned the men she hid were spies, she could have turned them over to win points with the king's guards. Instead, she lied to the king's men and, showing grace, helped the spies escape through her window by night.

I can't help but notice that Rahab's actions were a result of who she believed God to be. She made her choice to honor this God whom she had only heard about but who had chosen her, undeserving though she was. She served Him by saving the spies because of who He is. She believed in God's plan for the Israelites. She believed Him to be all-powerful. To be all-God. And she wanted to side with His plans. She trusted God to be victorious.

What if, when given the opportunity to forgive our enemies, we too could trust that God will be the victor? We needn't "settle the score" with those who hurt us but can trust God with the outcome. All we need to do is be the channels of His grace, trusting that He has the best plan for the future.

By faith Rahab hung the scarlet cord in her window, believing in the salvation only the Lord could provide. The scarlet cord, reminiscent of the blood painted on the doorposts of the homes of the Israelites before they fled Egypt. The scarlet cord that would save her and her family.

Did you notice that when the spies rescued her, that rescue was not contingent upon her promising to change her life of sin? She'd shown grace to the spies and, in turn, grace was shown to her. But since we know that she became the mother of Boaz, who married Ruth, who was King David's great-grandmother, it seems likely she *did* change—because once we have had the undeserved, unearned grace of God poured out over us, cleansing us of the shame and ugliness of our sin, why would we go back? We only want to move further into the arms of the Father of grace.

Like what my father did when I drove home, defeated, Father God held open His arms and drew Rahab in to bring her home into His family.

What a picture of grace she became, and that picture has extended well beyond her earthly life. By giving her a place of honor in the lineage of Jesus, God shows me that even the harlot is welcome home. Even the harlot has a place with Jesus. Even the harlot is cleansed of her shame and becomes an honored member of the family of God.

In the gift of grace, we can expect an encounter with God that we do not deserve and cannot earn. We cannot out-sin God's grace. There is no place I can go, no thing that I can do, that is bad enough or far enough to escape the grace of God.

SIX

Choices for the Wounded

One's philosophy is not best expressed in words. It is
expressed in choices one makes. In the long run, we
shape our lives ourselves. . . . And the choices we make
are ultimately our responsibility.

Eleanor Roosevelt

I was once in a small prayer group of dear women. We
shared things from our hearts and vowed to keep confidences. One day, a woman I'll call Chris shared in confidence
something dreadful that her husband had done. Some days
later I was talking with "Karen," a woman not in my prayer
group but who knew Chris. I told Karen what Chris had
shared. I shouldn't have—I broke confidence.

Immediately, I knew what I had done. I felt sick. The next
time I saw Chris I felt knots in my stomach. I knew I had to
confess to her what I had done and ask for her forgiveness.
I didn't want to do it—I dreaded doing so—but I knew I

would not be able to pretend everything was right between us until I did.

When we have wronged someone, most of us know it inside; our conscience tells us. It makes us uneasy to be around the person we hurt—even if they are not aware of the offense. Chris was unaware I had betrayed her confidence. But I was deeply aware. I believe the Holy Spirit was convicting me and wanted me to make it right not only with Chris but with the Lord Himself. The Holy Spirit is a spirit of truth, and when we offend others it is an offense to the Lord Himself. He desires for us to live in unity and loving truth with others.

I could have tried to pretend everything was okay, covered it over, and acted as if nothing was wrong. I admit that was tempting. Maybe I could have gone on for a long time pretending. Satan will tell us, *Ignore it; it will go away.* That is a lie. It won't go away. Remember what we said when wounds get buried alive—they come back later, when we least expect it. The same is true for sin. Breaking confidence with a friend is a sin—a betrayal of trust. The Holy Spirit, who lives within every believer, has a way of reminding us, pricking our conscience. Making us miserable until we obey His prompting. He doesn't let us get away with undealt-with sin that affects our relationship with Him. It is best to deal with it immediately.

I couldn't take back what I had said. The words had been spoken. I've heard that gossip is like throwing feathers into the wind. You can't gather them up again.

I, who knew so well what betrayal felt like, had done it myself. How could I have done that? How could have I been so insensitive? It was ugly. I didn't really want to look at it, much less tell another person. I had some choices to make.

For whenever we wrong someone else or are wronged, we have choices. As much as I didn't want to, I knew I had to tell the truth to myself, to God, and to Chris if I wanted to be free from the burden of guilt. Not make excuses. Not make light of it. Not skirt around it. I had to tell her the ugly truth that I had betrayed her confidence about a tender, private matter. Someone once said, "We give God permission to reshape our lives when we risk self-revelation and confession to others."[1]

I began with confession. I confessed my sin to God and asked His forgiveness, asking Him to cleanse me and make me right with Him. Then I asked Him to help me go to Chris and tell her and ask her forgiveness. That was the hard part. I pulled her aside after church one Sunday and confessed with tears what I had done. To look in her eyes and see the pain I had caused was difficult. I wanted to be anywhere but there, doing anything but this. Then I asked her forgiveness.

Chris was filled with grace and granted me her forgiveness. I was grateful.

Yet even then, Satan tried to tell me all sorts of lies. *She thinks less of you now. Chris will avoid you. What difference did it really make? Now you've made yourself vulnerable and she'll get back at you. She'll tell others you are not to be trusted.* He's clever. But I knew I had obeyed God, and I left the consequences with Him.

I renewed my mind with verses such as, "You desire truth in the innermost being" (Ps. 51:6), "By lovingkindness and truth iniquity is atoned for" (Prov. 16:6), "The truth will make you free" (John 8:32), and "He who practices the truth comes to the Light, so that his deeds may be manifested as having been wrought by God" (3:21). God's truth counteracts the subtleties of Satan's lies. God's Word is a powerful weapon to use.

After I renewed my mind, I felt it was important to tell Karen that I had been wrong and to ask for her forgiveness as well.

What began as wrongdoing on my part was transformed into a powerful experience of obedience and spiritual growth. And a huge part of that growth was due to the practice of confession.

Choose Confession

We have an enemy who tells us that confession is the last thing we want to do. He holds us hostage to the fear of what others will think of us. But we break his bondage when we confess our sins to God, to ourselves, and to those whom we have hurt. When we expose ourselves, the enemy can no longer dangle in front of us the fear of being exposed. When we choose confession, we are choosing freedom from our enemy's grasp.

Confess to God

I believe the place to start is always with personal confession to God. First John 1:9 tells us, "If we confess our sins, He is faithful and righteous to forgive us our sins and to cleanse us from all unrighteousness." That's a promise we can believe. God truly does wash us, cleansing us from the ugliness of our sin. Confession is the means by which we can maintain an open and honest relationship with our Father God. That clean and healthy relationship with God is the foundation from which we can then forgive ourselves and seek the forgiveness of others. You have the power of prayer and the Holy Spirit (if you have asked Jesus Christ to be your Lord and Savior) to help you. Once you've confessed to God, you take Him at His Word—He says you are forgiven. If the God of the whole universe says you are forgiven, then who are you to contradict Him? Thank Him for His complete forgiveness and move on to forgive yourself.

Forgive Yourself

What does it mean to forgive yourself? Those who study theology will say we do not have the spiritual authority to forgive ourselves. Only God can forgive us. But so many speak of "forgiveness of self." We all seem to know what it means but struggle to define it practically. My friend Jon Harris wrote to me in an email,

> I've read some who believe the Scripture never tells us to forgive ourselves . . . and I agree, but only if we're talking about using those particular words. But I firmly believe in forgiving any who have harmed us, and I certainly have harmed myself in varying ways over the years.

I'm with Jon. I've "harmed myself" in all manner of ways through my sinfulness, so "forgiving myself" has often proved to be very difficult, yet necessary, for me.

Maybe the difficulty is the terminology we use. When I speak of forgiving myself, I mean that I must learn to see myself the way God sees me—washed clean by the blood of Jesus. Only then can I accept the situation and move on, allowing me to accept myself.

We have an enemy who knows where we live and will do his best to keep us bound in fear and shame. But the chains can be broken.

So, how did I forgive myself, for instance, in the wake of my second marriage and divorce? Even after the baby steps taken in light of my father's "welcome home," I struggled with shame. After the hours, days, weeks, months, and possible years of denial, regret, shame, guilt—all the wasted time—how did I move on? After the anger, blame, shock, and misery, how did I move forward?

I had to say to myself, *I know this place of unforgiveness. It is well-worn. But I cannot stay here. It is damaging to my life, my psyche, my health . . . and it gets me nowhere.* Not forgiving myself damages my relationships with others and with myself. I cannot allow anyone to get close. I become negative. I cannot live in freedom. I always hold something back. Out of fear. Fear I will be rejected again. Fear I will prove to be inadequate. Fear I will be a disappointment. Fear I will be passed over. *Fear!*

Confess to Another Believer

Sometimes when I've struggled to let go of my regret and shame, I've found it useful to share the confession of my sin with another trusted believer. James 5:16 talks about confessing our sins to one another so that healing can take place. "Therefore, confess your sins to one another, and pray for one another so that you may be healed." I don't think James is referring solely to healing the body but the mind and emotions as well. He is talking about confessing to a real, live person. Confession is difficult and requires self-examination. It's a messy business. It is so humbling to admit your sins openly to someone else, be it a counselor, pastor, friend, or prayer partner.

We also have to be careful about whom we choose. It is important to find someone who is trustworthy, has spiritual understanding, and can keep a confidence. Mutual vulnerability is advisable and preferable. If no one comes to mind, ask God to show you who would be a wise confessor. As you pray, begin to observe those in your church or circle of influence, paying attention to those others trust—someone with a good track record.

Recently, my counselor asked me unexpectedly if I had subtly used my sexuality to attract men. I said yes. For the first time in my life, I'd admitted it to a real live person! And as I left his office, I felt happy! Happy that I was honest with him and myself. Yes, I had confessed this sin to God, many times, but there is something about face-to-face confession that is liberating. Proverbs 28:13 says, "He who conceals his transgressions will not prosper, but he who confesses and forsakes them will find compassion."

I do have two notes of caution when it comes to confession:

- Confess only your own stuff—not someone else's. It's easier to tell on someone else but that is not truth-telling, in this sense. It is being a tattletale!
- Don't confess to someone you've wronged just to clear your own conscience, like confessing to your spouse you have been unfaithful. That may make you feel better but devastate them. In such a case, confess

to your pastor or a more mature believer who can then help you navigate those rough waters. Confess in obedience to God.

Colossians 1:21–22 is a powerful passage to meditate on that will remind you of how God sees you, thanks to the blood of Jesus: "And although you were formerly alienated and hostile in mind, engaged in evil deeds, yet He has now reconciled you in His fleshly body through death, in order to present you before Him holy and blameless and beyond reproach." You are reconciled to God. He sees you as holy and blameless and beyond reproach! Amazing!

Choose to Ask Forgiveness

After confessing your sins to God and asking His forgiveness, it's time to ask the one you wounded for forgiveness. Some of us can go around in circles for days, weeks, months—even years—avoiding this important practice. Could that be you? Maybe you thought the wrong you did was long buried and forgotten. But if one day you remember what you did and feel a conviction by the Holy Spirit to make it right, I encourage you to take the bold step and ask forgiveness. Notice here that you aren't confessing to the one you've wronged in order to earn forgiveness from God or yourself. You've now already been forgiven by God and yourself.

As with confession, I have found that the enemy helps me make excuses and rationalizations so that I remain in disobedience. Satan is very clever and successful in his tactics. He will bring all manner of things to mind as reasons you shouldn't do it. *What will they think of me? They will take revenge. I don't want to make myself vulnerable. It's too painful. It's not really necessary; they don't remember what I did.* Another of his tactics is to convince us that asking forgiveness is hard and complicated. The best way I have found is to simply do it. Yes, asking for forgiveness is hard because it is humbling, but there is no complicated formula. Here are a few tips I have found helpful.

First, remember that when we commit to obey Jesus, He comes to our aid and helps us do all things He requires of us. We needn't do anything—including forgiveness—under our own steam. The Holy Spirit is there to help us, even with the words we say.

Second, also remember that when we're putting off something we are dreading, we'll never simply come across the "perfect" time to get it done. There are times I have had to pick up the phone and make an appointment with someone to ask for forgiveness. With Chris, I knew when I'd see her next, so I committed to speak to her then. In other situations, I have been more spontaneous.

Third, I recommend that, whenever possible, speak to the person face-to-face. If that's not possible, arrange a phone call. (An email is not the way to do it—you are not facing the situation openly.) Greet them warmly. You can make small talk for a few minutes but don't get sidetracked. For example, I said, "Chris, I want to ask for your forgiveness for betraying your confidence by telling someone else about your secret. I can only imagine the pain I've caused you. I knew it was wrong and I am very sorry. Will you forgive me?"

Fourth, this encounter is not the time to mention any ways they may have hurt you. Your focus is on your own sin, not theirs. Be very careful not to blame. Don't say, "You did this . . ." Keep the confession and request short and to the point. Don't go down rabbit trails. Be specific, never vague. Don't say, "If I hurt you." Simply say, "I did this. It was wrong. I'm sorry. Will you forgive me?"

Fifth, realize people respond in many different ways. Very often the person is more than willing to forgive and healing begins. Some people don't know what to say and try to change the subject. Don't let them brush it off as, "No big deal." It is a big deal to you, and you are asking their forgiveness. You can redirect sweetly and say, "I am really asking you to forgive me for betraying you. I am so sorry. Will you forgive me?"

Some will not be able to respond. Don't try to force it. You cannot ask someone to give you something they do not have in them to give. Be gracious and thank them for being willing to talk with you. And go on your way. You were obedient, and God will honor that. There may be a day they come to you and revisit the conversation. Give them the freedom to do that.

Some people may get angry and ask questions, wanting details. Others may handle their anger by venting. Realize they have their own emotions to deal with. They may be hearing this for the first time and need a moment to catch up. You may have to let them process it and then come back to it by telling them something like, "I understand if you need some time to think about and process this." You're not asking them to stuff their emotions or pretend they aren't struggling with what you have revealed to them. Rely on the Holy Spirit as to how much to say and stay focused. This isn't a time to get into an argument nor to be defensive or offer excuses. Your focus is on your wrong and your hope for forgiveness.

Finally, realize that although you are acting in obedience, you don't have guarantees of positive results. You can only do your part, not control the response of another person. The results are God's and God's alone. Trust Him. Whatever they say, that's their "stuff." God will honor your obedience. He really will. And no matter what the other person does, you can rely on God's forgiveness, which is 100 percent guaranteed by the blood of Jesus.

Choose to Be Forgiving

We've spent five chapters exploring much about the meaning, the motivation, and the foundation of forgiveness. We have much more to discover in the pages ahead about giving and receiving forgiveness and overcoming the hurdles and roadblocks that seem to keep forgiveness beyond our grasp, but here in the context of our choices of confession and seeking forgiveness, let's focus on just one aspect: the choice *to pray to be a forgiving person.* I remember what I felt when Chris forgave me: relief. And when Daddy welcomed me home with an embrace that told me I was forgiven, I felt safe and accepted. I hope that you can recall similar experiences, enough to know that you want to be the kind of person who extends forgiveness to others.

If we *willfully refuse* to forgive another for the wrong they have done us, then perhaps we have not truly repented of our own sins. That is worth exploring. Forgiveness and mercy are telltale signs of our walk with Jesus. Keep in mind here I am not talking about a *struggle* to forgive—that is fine and honest! It may be why you bought this book. I am talking about making a determined decision to *refuse* to be obedient to God by deliberately choosing not to forgive. If we knowingly withhold forgiveness, it's good to spend time at the foot of the cross. By this I mean revisiting the truth that Jesus died once for the forgiveness of sin and offers that forgiveness to all of us freely.

Consider Matthew 18:35, "My heavenly Father will also do the same to you, if each of you does not forgive his brother from your heart." Forgiveness must be from the heart and be sincere. Outwardly, we can fake forgiveness. But God sees our heart. Don't be alarmed if it seems impossible to forgive. It takes time. Step by step, it is a process. If God knows our heart is to forgive, He is not going to hold it against us if we are in an honest struggle in that direction. So what we can do, even if we have not yet arrived at a point of forgiveness for a specific wrong done to us, is *set our face toward forgiveness.* Make the choice to be a forgiving person, even if we cannot find a way to do it yet in a specific instance.

How do we get started? By choosing to pray to that end. Don't worry about the feelings or the roadblocks. Begin to pray. Honestly ask God to help you. It probably will not happen suddenly. It's a process—often gradual—that God orchestrates in His time.

You can start with a simple prayer like this: *Lord, I want to forgive others just as You have forgiven me, but I realize I'm not there yet. I confess the unforgiveness in my heart. I ask that You change my heart, soften it, so that I can grow into being the forgiving person You want me to be. With Your help, Lord, I want to now enter into the process of forgiveness honestly and earnestly. In Jesus's name, Amen.*

Choose to Discern If Reconciliation Is in Order

To reconcile means to restore to friendship or harmony.[2] No one enjoys severed relationships. They are hard on everyone. How many families have been devastated by a fracture and then stubbornly refused to forgive or seek reconciliation? One family member holds on to their hurt and viewpoint, rejecting any other views. It can go on for years—maybe so long that members of the family forget what the fracture was even about. I remember being in Northern Ireland and asking a gentleman there what all the fighting was about, which had lasted for thirty years, from 1968 to 1998. Hundreds had been killed or maimed. Fear had run in the streets. He looked at me, nonplussed, and said he really couldn't remember! How terribly sad.

A gentleman I was dating one summer declared his love for me. I knew him to be a very kind and gentle man, and though we enjoyed spending time with each other, I wasn't in love with him. I then decided to move to Florida to get a new start and be near my sister and a good church. We stayed in touch. Then I entered into my rebound marriage, and it hurt this gentleman deeply.

When that marriage fell apart, I eventually returned to Virginia. A mutual friend urged me to contact the man. I refused. I knew I had hurt him and did not think it would be wise to open an old wound. Then my friend orchestrated a phone call between us.

I knew I had to ask his forgiveness. During the call he was at first a bit stern but when I specifically asked for his forgiveness, he granted it. We chatted briefly, and I hung up knowing that all was forgiven. Not too long after that call one of my daughters, who enjoyed him, asked if he could come for dinner. He did. We began to date and over time fell in love and married. That marriage lasted almost ten years before, sadly, it ended in divorce. However, we remain friends to this day and often go to the movies together. He sometimes joins my children and me for holiday dinners.

Appropriate reconciliation is a beautiful thing. It creates harmony and reestablishes community. Peace follows true, healthy reconciliation and allows spiritual growth to continue.

God has provided us with the ultimate picture of reconciliation. As it says in Colossians 1:21–22, "And although you were formerly alienated and hostile in mind, engaged in evil deeds, yet He has now reconciled you in His fleshly body through death, in order to present you before Him holy and blameless and beyond reproach."

It is critically important, however, that we never confuse forgiveness with reconciliation. As we discussed in chapter 3, forgiveness is not the same as reconciliation. Forgiveness is unconditional. Reconciliation is conditional. Reconciliation requires an agreement between two parties. Forgiveness must take place first, then the possibilities of reconciliation can be explored. Author June Hunt says it well.

> Forgiveness requires no relationship. However, reconciliation requires a relationship in which two people, in agreement, are walking toward the same goal. . . . Forgiveness involves a change in thinking about the offender. Reconciliation involves a change in behavior by the offender.[3]

For instance, Chris, whose confidence I had broken, forgave me. That didn't mean that she was obligated to trust me again. Thankfully, she chose to do so by continuing to share her confidences with the group when I was present, demonstrating that she was reconciled with me, and, in turn, I never broke her confidence again. We were reconciled. My gentleman friend forgave me, and over time we reconciled and eventually married. Even after our divorce we experienced forgiveness, and though we never remarried we reconciled as friends and maintain a lovely friendship to this day.

I like how Laura Waters Hinson put it: "Forgiveness asks you to give up your right to be angry, reconciliation asks you to enter back into relationship with the people you have forgiven."[4] Trust is not necessarily a by-product of forgiveness. The thinking that says that once you have forgiven you are required to reconcile is a mistaken notion about forgiveness that is often used to bludgeon the wounded. As pastor Rick Warren writes, "Trust must be rebuilt over time. Trust requires a track record."[5]

When I was so wounded after learning of my first husband's infidelities, there were some in the church who pressured me to reunite with him. That was another wounding piled on top of the wounds I had already endured in our fractured relationship. Could people not see the damage that had been done over the years? We didn't have a strong foundation upon which to rebuild. In the three years that passed between my learning of his infidelity and my decision to divorce, I was at times hopeful as I explored the possibility of restored trust, but in the end I had to recognize that though I could forgive, we could not be reconciled.

Sadly, he died eight years after our divorce. Had he lived longer, we might have become friends as we matured, our children became adults, and the grandchildren came along.

He would have loved to watch his grandchildren grow up, for he loved children. He'd be so proud of them today. As for my second husband, whom I feared, on the advice of my wise pastor and others, I never spoke to him again. It was best for me to remove myself and work through forgiveness alone with God and my counselor. God has healed that memory. He too has since died.

Many people try to rush reconciliation because it makes everything look neat and tidy. And because it seems to be proof that we actually forgave. If we don't reconcile, we fear others will think we haven't forgiven. The church loves neat and tidy—it looks good and we like the image it presents. We are, after all, image keepers of the best sort. We like to demonstrate that faith in Jesus really works. How tempting to make believe that we are living victoriously. Reconciliation looks God-honoring on the outside, but it isn't if it is rushed or is a pretense that forces us to put on a mask and live inauthentically. Reconciliation can only be accomplished if and when the wounded party is ready—no sooner. That may be a slow process, if reconciliation can happen at all.

With that understanding, once forgiveness has been granted, make the choice to consider whether reconciliation would be wise, healthy, and possible. If so, explore moving in that direction, but I recommend seeking wise counsel in that process, especially when one's health, welfare, and safety are a consideration. Specifically, in abusive relationships it is sometimes unwise to reconcile. We have a spiritual responsibility to protect ourselves and our children. How wonderful to realize in those situations, however, that one can experience the freedom of forgiveness even in the absence of reconciliation.

Choose to Take Your Emotions to God in Prayer

We've discussed four major choices to work through when we've been wounded. Finally, let's look at one choice that I believe has the power to absolutely transform our experience of forgiveness. It is a choice modeled by Jesus at the single most critical point in His life.

Jesus too had choices in forgiveness. He didn't have to go to the cross. The Bible says He despised the shame of it. "Christ redeemed us from the curse of the Law, having become a curse for us—for it is written, 'Cursed is everyone who hangs on a tree'" (Gal. 3:13). Another word for "despise" is *loathe*. Jesus loathed the thought of it. He loathed the curse of it. He loathed the humiliation of it. He loathed the pain of it. He had a choice. He didn't have to die on the cross and become the curse, enduring the pain and humiliation. He could have told His Father it was too great a price. But "He was journeying with His face toward Jerusalem" (Luke 9:53). He determined to fulfill God's plan of redemption begun before the world was made. (It blows my mind that God had a plan even before mankind was created!)

Throughout Jesus's lifetime, the forces of darkness pulled on Him. He never got a break from the shadow of the cross; it followed Him from His birth until it literally loomed over Him as He stumbled up Golgotha's hill.

But before He got to Golgotha, He visited a garden. It was Jesus's habit to withdraw from the crowd and sometimes even withdraw from His disciples to pray; to commune with God, His Father.

It would have been fun, I suppose, to eavesdrop on His prayers throughout His ministry. I'm sure Jesus and His Father talked about everything.

103

"Father do You think I should call Matthew or Andrew?"

"Call both. They will be good disciples."

"Father, what should I do about Peter's impulsivity?"

"Don't worry about it; Peter will be a great leader. I have plans for him."

"Father, I am tired."

"Son, I know You are; come and rest. Let Me take the burden."

"Father, Lazarus died! I should have gone right away to heal him so he wouldn't have died. I am so sad for Mary and Martha."

"I know You are, Son, but You are going to show My glory in a powerful way when You raise him from death. Remember, You are the resurrection and the life."

"Father, these people are so much to deal with! They are noisy. They stink!"

"Son, You are human like they are so that I will understand what it is to be human. And, Son, there are times You smell too!"

On the night before His crucifixion, after the supper in the upper room, Jesus told His disciples that they would all leave Him, but after He was raised from the dead He would see them in Galilee. I am sure they didn't comprehend what He was really talking about. They all declared they would remain true, including Peter, who was adamant about his loyalty. He said he would die for Jesus. Jesus told Peter he would deny Him three times before dawn.

Then Jesus and His disciples (except Judas, who had already departed) went across to the Kidron Valley at the base of the Mount of Olives to the garden called Gethsemane. He told His disciples to pray while He went a little farther beyond in order to pray alone. He took Peter, James, and John and asked them to keep watch with Him while He prayed. He told them He was very grieved, to the point of death. Did they not wonder what was going on? Did they not see His distress? Were they so self-focused? Were they that tired?

Then He went a bit farther, fell on His face and began to talk to His Father. We don't know the full content of His prayer, only bits of it, probably overheard by John. And how did John hear it? Jesus was not silent. He was agonizing aloud in prayer. The book of Hebrews tells us, "He offered up both prayers and supplications with loud crying and tears to the One able to save Him from death" (Heb. 5:7). He cried out to God, "My Father, if it is possible, let this cup pass from Me; yet not as I will, but as You will" (Matt. 26:39).

Jesus was struggling with the whole idea of crucifixion. He didn't want it. Everything in His humanness fought against it. He was in a battle of epic and eternal proportions. Not only was all of hell fighting Him but surely He had to battle the anger He felt toward those who were soon to lie about Him during the trial, the ones who plotted behind His back, the ones who would hammer the nails through His hands. All the humiliation He would feel at His nakedness. The shame He would feel being crucified on a cross. All the revenge He could dish out. All the sadness. All the heartbreak. The war was raging in Him. My friend Dr. Terry Wardle wrote, "That anguish was the outpouring of emotional stress, anticipating betrayal, rejection, mockery, abuse, ending in a savage death.

Jesus did not vent this toward His offenders, but poured out His feelings before the Father."[6]

Jesus took a break to find the disciples—and they were sleeping! His agony was being played out only a few feet away, and they had fallen asleep. "So, you men could not keep watch with Me for one hour?" He asked (v. 40). His closest friends could not stay awake to "be there" for Him. Although He knew their weakness and that they were tired, His deep, cosmic loneliness had begun. Jesus then cautioned them to be vigilant about temptation because He knew they may be willing to obey God, but their nature was weak, and they might give in to it. He knew only too well they would.

He went back to pray. This time He did not ask for the ordeal of crucifixion to be taken from Him but chose His Father's will over His own. He would obey even at such a price. A price He hated. Again, He sought out His disciples, and again they were sleeping. He left the sleeping disciples and went back to pray a third time. He prayed the same thing: "Your will be done" (v. 42). He yielded and surrendered to God's plan and will. How did He do that? He made the choice. Just as Jesus "set His face toward Jerusalem," He determined to choose to obey His Father even into the cruel death of crucifixion. It was a powerful determination that all of hell tried to hinder.

The next day, with all of His body an open, oozing, bloody wound, they nailed Him to the cross. Taunted Him. Mocked Him. Jeered and made fun of Him. Gambled for His only earthly belonging—His robe. And as the nails were pounded into His wrists, He uttered, "Father, forgive them; for they do not know what they are doing" (Luke 23:34).

How could He pray such a prayer? He could have called legions of angels to obliterate those soldiers—and everyone else—on that craggy hill outside of Jerusalem. He chose not to. He could have called on His Father to save Him from the agony and humiliation. He chose not to. He was not out for vengeance. How could He have forgiven so completely?

He had done His homework on His knees!

On His knees in the garden, He had vented to His Father all His powerful emotions and battled them in prayer. And, indeed, He felt all His emotions as a human.

> Only after unloading the agonizing emotional and spiritual turmoil did Jesus offer forgiveness to those who crucified Him. . . . Jesus let His emotions spill out before God. As a result, when from the cross He said, "Father forgive them, for they do not know what they are doing" (Luke 23:34), there was no hidden bitterness or resentment. He had already surrendered His hurt to God during those hours of emotional anguish.[7]

The same choice Jesus had is available to us. By the Holy Spirit who lives within us, we are able to do as Jesus did—forgive the most heinous crimes against us. Like the missionary in Nepal forgave his grandson's murderer. Is it easy? No! Is it simple? Yes. We can follow His example with His power living in us. On our own, in our humanness, it is impossible. But we do have His power available to us!

I have never suffered as Jesus did. Nor have any of us. He told us to forgive the impossible, then showed us how when He settled it before the cross. He settled it in Gethsemane. He agonized with His Father. He got His emotions out. He

107

wasn't passive. As physician Luke tells us in his Gospel, "His sweat became like drops of blood" (Luke 22:44). This is a condition known as hematidrosis. It occurs when, under great stress, tiny capillaries in the sweat glands break, mixing blood and sweat.[8]

Jesus knew the safest place to vent. He knew the only help He had was in God. He spilled His emotions in prayer in the garden so that He wouldn't take revenge and could forgive. All the anger, hurt, and bitterness He would feel, He poured out to God then. And that's a safe place to pour it all out. Otherwise we pour it out on people.

Prayer is the safe place—that safe place between you and God where you can say it all.

Let us follow Jesus's example—He told His Dad!

SEVEN

The Call for Help

You and I will fail, but we are not failures. We are sons and daughters of the living God, heirs of the resources of the kingdom that will never end.

Dr. Terry Wardle

I have a painting by my sweet friend, artist Carolyn Blish, which hangs in my bedroom. It is a picture of Jesus with His face to the storm as His arm is stretched out to calm it. I love that painting. It reminds me of the power of the storm and the greater power of my God.

Whatever storm has blown into your life and left you struggling with forgiveness, God is available to help you. Just as He was there for Jesus in the Garden of Gethsemane, He is listening for you to ask Him to help. He wants to help us.

You can cry out with the psalmist:

> I will lift up my eyes to the mountains;
> From where shall my help come?
> My help comes from the LORD,
> Who made heaven and earth. (Ps. 121:1–2)

Do you find it hard to ask for help? I do. Why is asking for help so hard for some of us? In our Western culture, we highly value independence. We like to think we can solve any problem ourselves. When something unexpected happens in my life, my first response is to keep a brave, "I can handle this" face on and see what I can do to fix it. I tire myself out trying to take care of everything while I take pride in being self-sufficient and independent. I don't want to ask for help. I don't like being needy. I don't want to be obligated to anyone. I don't want to put anyone out.

A few years ago, I found myself stranded on an interstate, alone and in the dark. Even then, at first I didn't call for help. Until I had to.

The Deer in the Headlights

The fog was a dense gray blanket over the Blue Ridge Mountains early that October morning. My flight to New York was the first one out of the local airport, then I would go on to Maine, where I would visit my college roommate for the weekend. I was looking forward to this "girls' time" away as I jumped out of bed, made my cup of tea, finished packing, and anticipated a great time together.

It usually takes me fifty minutes to get to the airport. I try to time everything just right in order to make my flights on time, taking into account all the variables I can think of.

This particular morning I assumed nothing would go wrong. Certainly, I wouldn't encounter traffic at that early hour. I was on schedule.

The car seemed cozy as I carefully drove through the fog on Interstate 64. I had the radio tuned to the news and weather. The "super storm" Sandy was just making the news for the weekend, but it did not sound as if it was going to affect my travel. I would be well out of its path. My old car, a Volvo wagon, felt safe and comfortable.

Then, as I drove up a gentle slope in the road, out of the fog, like a gray ghost, stepped a deer. Right in front of me. I didn't have time to think. I didn't even swerve. I broadsided it. Blam! I didn't run over it. I didn't even see it in the roadway afterward. It must have run away, wounded as it was.

I had never hit a deer or been a passenger in a car that had hit one. I did not know what to do. My car was still running, and since I was far from the airport or any lights, and no other cars were nearby, I decided to keep on driving even though all sorts of warning lights were flashing on my instrument panel.

I was shaken and sad. I had taken such good care of my eleven-year-old car, and now it was damaged. Soon the instrument panel blazed with a bright red warning light that seemed to shout, "Stop the car now!" I pulled to the side of the road and wondered, *Now what do I do?* My mind began to race. I would never make my flight on time. I had to notify the airline to cancel my seat. I had to call my college roommate in Maine to tell her the change of plans. But then who should I call? I realized I needed help. I was all alone and stranded in the dark. Was this an appropriate 9-1-1 call? Surely, if it wasn't, they would know what to do. I hesitated

111

for a few minutes, then finally dialed 9-1-1 and realized with a surge of fear that my phone battery was nearly dead.

When the dispatcher answered, I told her what had happened. Immediately she asked if I was okay. I hadn't even thought about that! The airbags had not deployed, and I assured her I was fine. She patched me through to the state police. I repeated the situation to an officer and he too quickly asked if I was all right. He asked my location and where the deer was. I told him the deer was long gone as far as I knew and gave him the approximate location where I'd pulled over onto the shoulder.

To my relief it wasn't long before I saw flashing blue lights in the distance and a trooper pulled up behind me. Soon I saw a fire truck and ambulance also headed my way. It seemed like much ado about nothing. I was okay. But when the tow truck arrived and my poor wounded car was loaded on its flatbed, I had to face the fact that I was not getting to the airport anytime soon.

I had just enough power left in my cell phone to call my daughter Noelle. To my amazement she told me she was on the same interstate, headed my way. She "happened" to be meeting her running group early that morning. Noelle took me back home. I rented a car, and with just a bit of a delay, I was off for Maine. By God's providence He'd provided all the help I needed. I was so grateful that I hadn't been left alone to fend for myself.

I've read about soldiers wounded in battle. There are those who see themselves as tough and strong and don't want to admit they are hit, embarrassed they need help. Believing themselves to be invulnerable and indestructible, when asked how they are, they reply, "I'm okay." They deny the wound—maybe try to hide it from others—until they are forced to acknowledge their need. Such a soldier may even angrily fight off anyone wanting to help him. He wants to be in control. He is proud and hates to face the reality of the injury. But he is now afraid. He has to recognize he is not invincible. He is supposed to be the one who comes to the rescue, not the one who needs rescuing. Eventually though, if he is to get the healing he needs, he must accept help.

Then there are those who, like the deer, take off running after being hit. They keep moving forward as if nothing had happened. Adrenaline kicks in and they keep going until the wound kills them. Few ask for assistance. Rare it is for one of these men to say, "I have been wounded. Please help me."

I don't want to be like that, yet I find it scary to realize I am not in control and have to be dependent on others. I'm not good at it. But that day on the mountain, when faced with no other option than to receive help, I was very grateful for that state trooper, the tow truck driver, and especially Noelle.

Our Helper in the Battle

In the previous chapter, Jesus set a wonderful example for us at Gethsemane. He was the Son of God, yet even He called out for help in prayer. Forgiveness, as we have discussed, seems impossible at times—beyond our ability. The truth is we cannot do it without help. God knew that would be our condition, so He provided help for us. In John 14:16, Jesus said, "I will ask the Father, and He will give you another Helper, that He may be with you forever." That Helper is the Holy Spirit.

The word *helper* means more than one who offers assistance. It means *advocate*, as in a legal setting. An advocate is one who will stand with us and take our side. The Holy Spirit, as our advocate, pleads for us. He is One who is stronger, more articulate, and more knowledgeable, and He will enable us to do what God has commanded. When we have this kind of advocate with us in our times of anger, bitterness, rage, fear, and anxiety, it is a huge comfort. As a matter of fact, the word *helper* also means *comforter*—one who understands, cares, listens, assures, and encourages.

The Holy Spirit is not just a warm, fuzzy feeling. He is God's power living in us. Without His power we cannot live the Christian life. Without His power we certainly cannot generate transformational forgiveness. Without the Holy Spirit, all the self-effort, all the "turning the page," all the new beginnings will come to nothing. No matter how much energy we throw at living a spiritual life or how much we may know about it, we cannot produce a healthy Christian life under our own power. It is only as Christ's power flows through us from His Spirit that we are able to fully experience the Christian life.

Perhaps this is best understood by Jesus's own illustration of the branches and the vine in John 15. He says He is the vine and we are the branches. We have to stay attached to the vine for our life-giving sustenance. The Holy Spirit is like the sap that flows up from the source, through the vine to the branches. If a branch is cut off from the vine's life source, it withers and dies. However, as long as it remains in the vine, the life-giving sap keeps it alive and fresh.

Forgiveness is far more than a challenge. It is a battle. Often, as we explored in the previous chapter, we must battle just to make the choice to be forgiving. But when it comes to the call to forgive a gross injustice or grievous wound done to us, it is a battle of the will. We often don't *want* to forgive. And once we clear that hurdle, we may still find that, on our own, the capacity for forgiveness is beyond our grasp.

Thankfully, we do not need to battle alone. Our decision to forgive is the doorway for the Holy Spirit to inhabit and empower that decision. Otherwise we will attempt to forgive on our own, become frustrated, make a bigger mess, or try to ignore it. Yes, as we seek to forgive those who wound us, we enter a spiritual battlefield.

We use the word *battle* often in our culture. We battle drug wars; we battle floods and fires; we battle poverty. We are familiar with the term. Those battles and others like them are separate from us, exterior battles. But forgiveness is an inner battle. It is a spiritual battle. A battle of the heart and will.

Never forget that we have an enemy who doesn't follow any rules of engagement. He is cunning, subtle, ruthless, a liar, and is always looking for a weak spot to attack. The Bible says, "Your adversary, the devil, prowls around like a roaring lion, seeking someone to devour" (1 Pet. 5:8). He hates us. He is not a cartoon character dressed in red with horns, a long tail, and a pitchfork. He is deadly. He has to be taken seriously because he takes *you* seriously.

There have been many misunderstandings about who the Holy Spirit is and what He does. I recently talked with a friend who seemed surprised to hear that the Holy Spirit was a person we can pray to, the third Person of the Trinity: Father, Son, and Holy Spirit. He is God. So, who is the Holy Spirit and what does He do? As a Christian, you have the Holy Spirit within you. He comes in when we ask Jesus into our hearts and lives and become believing Christians. We have God living in us. Let that sink in a minute.

God's Spirit lives in us. He makes all His power and wisdom available to us for living this Christian life. What if we took that seriously?

He is far more powerful than the devil. And His power is available to us as we seek to forgive those who have wounded us or we seek to forgive ourselves. The Holy Spirit convicts us to move in obedience to what God would have us do. He is a permanent, eternal, not-going-anywhere helper for us. It is not my purpose here to teach the doctrine of the Holy Spirit. That is a huge subject that has been taught and written about many times over by far brighter folks than me. But we need to be aware that God has given us a supernatural power and help in the person of the Holy Spirit.

He is *with* us in fellowship, *by* us in personal presence, and *in* us with His personal energy. He strengthens us and gives us courage. We need those things as we go through the process of forgiveness. It takes strength to persist; it takes courage to humble ourselves and ask for forgiveness and enter the process of forgiving another. It is simple, but it isn't easy. Daily, if not hourly, we have to ask for His power to help us when everything in us screams, *No, I don't want to!*

An Explosion of Anger

Right after I learned of my first husband's infidelity, I told my pastor I was not angry or hurt. I didn't feel angry. I didn't look angry. Oh, but I was. Betrayal cuts deep, and that's where my anger was hiding.

As I was growing up, I never saw angry people. I never heard my mother and father argue. I remember once telling my mother I was angry about something and she told me we shouldn't be angry. Anger was not acceptable in our home. So what was I to do with the anger I felt? I didn't know.

It took months for the anger I felt at my husband's betrayal to come out because I stuffed it far down inside in order to "look" like I was handling it. But I couldn't keep it there for long. One afternoon the anger roared out. Our pastor and his wife came by with their kids to swim in the pool. We were relaxed and having fun until something triggered my submerged anger. I exploded all over my husband. I didn't care who heard me or what I said. I was blinded by fury. My pastor wisely ushered us into the house and took the kids with them to their home. I raged against my husband for quite some time, until the anger and I were both spent.

Then I justified my actions. *This was his fault. He's the one who betrayed me. I wouldn't have lit into him if he hadn't provoked it. He deserved it!* I felt I was within my rights to get angry and lash out and inflict pain. I wanted to punish him, make him hurt as much as I did.

In spite of the fact that I was justifying myself, however, in reality I regretted my behavior. It wasn't like me to be angry. I'm not an angry person in general. I felt convicted for how I'd mishandled my anger. I realized I had not been honest with myself about what I was feeling. I had just stuffed my anger until it detonated.

The last thing I wanted to do, however, was ask for my husband's forgiveness! After all, he was the one who'd been unfaithful. Why should I have to apologize to him for anything?

I began to compartmentalize so I didn't have to think about it. Yes, I could teach that Bible class—my hurt and anger were tucked away. We keep the pain we have caused (or that was inflicted on us) in just one area of our heart and mind so it cannot spill over into other areas of our life and thoughts. It is a coping mechanism to keep our anger at bay, but not a healthy one.

My husband died before I ever asked for his forgiveness for that incident. But that didn't mean I was off the hook. I have since talked to God about it, confessed it, and asked His forgiveness. And I've even asked God to tell my husband how sorry I am for how I treated him in my woundedness. I'm not sure if that is theologically correct, but God knows my heart . . . I'll let Him sort it out.

Looking back, I see the Holy Spirit at work, convicting me and inspiring me to ask forgiveness. *Conviction* is a word we use a lot in the Christian world. But what does it really mean? Well, it is not shame, though I think we often confuse the two. The Holy Spirit's conviction does not bring shame. It is actually a gift from Him. Conviction from the Holy Spirit is positive and comes as a prodding or nudging—a persistent voice in our mind—that reminds us of a truth and urges us to obey. Conviction causes us to feel uncomfortable or unsettled until we are spurred to action, especially if we neglect to obey or put off doing the right thing. It may grow louder if ignored, motivating us to reach toward God, who wants the absolute best for you and me. And that best includes giving and receiving forgiveness.

When we feel convicted, we have some choices to make. Let's take a look at two of Jesus's disciples and the choices they made when they realized they had failed their Lord.

Judas and Peter: Two Responses When Forgiveness Was Needed

Judas Iscariot was one of the twelve disciples. He walked with the Lord for three years all over the countryside and from city to city. He heard Jesus preach the Sermon on the Mount. He witnessed the multiplication of the loaves and fishes for the hungry crowd and helped gather up the leftovers. He was in the boat when the storm arose on the Sea of Galilee and saw the wind and waves obey Jesus. It's hard to understand how he could experience all of that firsthand yet still betray the Lord.

Perhaps he followed Jesus for what he could get out of it. His was a shallow commitment to Jesus. Jesus wasn't what Judas wanted or expected. He wanted a conquering hero, one who would lead the revolt against Rome to free Israel from oppression. He wanted a Messiah of power, might, and victory. He wanted to be in that parade as one of Jesus's "cabinet members." Had he suppressed his true feelings of anger and bitterness and greed? Did he have questions about Jesus's purpose and mission? Did his questions cause doubt?

Undoubtedly, he heard the questions religious leaders asked Jesus and knew they doubted too. Maybe he began to stand closer to them and farther from Jesus when the crowds drew close. He might have heard their murmured comments and escalating hatred. Maybe it fed his own disillusionment and frustration. Maybe he overheard their angry words among themselves and their plans to trap Jesus. "The chief priests and the scribes were seeking how they might put Him to death; for they were afraid of the people" (Luke 22:2).

Judas knew Jesus's plan to celebrate the Passover with His disciples. He knew the places Jesus frequented in order to get alone to pray. "And he went away and discussed with the chief priests and officers how he might betray Him to them" (v. 4). The religious leaders knew him to be a follower of Jesus and were curious that he approached them. In his eager greed, he must have asked them how much they would pay him to turn Jesus over to them. They were more than willing to welcome Judas and his betrayal. They came to an agreement. "They were glad and agreed to give him money" (v. 5). He began to look for the right opportunity and time.

We don't read in the Scriptures if Judas struggled with his choice. Even after his meeting with the religious leaders and his agreement with them, he was still in Jesus's company—still one of the disciples. He still had time to repent. At the Last Supper in the upper room, when Jesus dipped the bread in the wine and handed it to Judas, it was a moment of grace. But Judas's heart was hardened and he didn't respond to the offered grace. Jesus even said, "But behold, the hand of the one betraying Me is with Mine on the table" (v. 21). Judas would not receive the truth Jesus spoke and did not tell himself the truth about his own greed and ambition. There were so many opportunities for him to come clean over the years—even that last night together with Jesus—but he was self-deceived.

Perhaps Judas thought that in the end Jesus would not be convicted, or, if He was, He would slip through the hands of the religious leaders as He had many times before when the crowd got out of control. In his deceived mind, he may have thought Jesus would confound the leaders and be freed, and Judas would be the richer for it. But his plans went all

120

wrong. Apparently, after Jesus was condemned, Judas had a change of mind. He realized this was going further than he ever thought. Jesus was innocent. He knew that. The Scripture says, "Satan entered into Judas" (v. 3). For Judas to betray the One who loved him so, it had to be the work of Satan.

Judas, filled with anguish and grief, took steps toward repentance. He tried to undo it. He took the money back to the elders, but it was too late; Jesus was condemned. Judas confessed his sin, but to men, not to God. These religious leaders turned on him, indifferent to his suffering. They used him for their own agenda, then rejected him. He was desperate and felt totally alone in his anguish. He saw the enormity and horror of what he had done but he did not remember all Jesus's words about God's mercy and love. He forgot and could not see the grace of God. He felt he had out-sinned God's mercy. Judas's god was too small—a god who was not merciful and gracious and forgiving. Judas didn't think God could or would forgive him. The Bible says, simply and solemnly, "And he threw the pieces of silver into the temple sanctuary and departed; and he went away and hanged himself" (Matt. 27:5). What a tragic story.

In contrast, there is Peter. We all love the apostle Peter! Impetuous, he was the one who got out of the boat to walk on the water to Jesus. He was outspoken. He was the first disciple to declare Jesus was the Son of God. He was a natural leader, taking the other disciples fishing after the resurrection. He loved Jesus, vowing he would die for Him. When Jesus was being arrested in the garden, Peter drew his sword to defend him. He followed Jesus into the court of the high priest that night. And yet he weakened out of fear for his own skin and denied Jesus not once, not twice, but three times, swearing he didn't know Him. The Gospel of Luke tells us, "The Lord turned and looked at Peter. And Peter remembered the word of the Lord, how He had told him, 'before a rooster crows today, you will deny Me three times'" (Luke 22:61).

Peter knew in that one look that Jesus knew what Peter had done.

In that look, the reality of recognition was disclosed. Peter knew that no man had ever loved him as Jesus did. The Man whom he had confessed as the Christ, the Son of the living God, looked into his eyes, saw the transparent terror there, watched him act out the dreadful drama of his security addiction, and loved him. The love of Jesus for Peter lay in his complete and unconditional acceptance of him.[1]

I cannot imagine what Peter must have felt. Deep regret. Punishing guilt. If only he could take the words back. If only he had not gone into the high priest's house. The Bible says, "And he went out and wept bitterly" (v. 62).

What is the difference between Judas and Peter? Judas could not accept the grace of God offered to him. He could not see the goodness of God. He could not stand himself. He hanged himself immediately. He didn't think he could go confess to the others. He took matters into his own hands, not trusting God's love and grace.

Peter wept bitterly. That led to repentance. We don't know what happened next with Peter. He wasn't named at the crucifixion, so it's probable he wasn't there. Maybe he was too ashamed. Or maybe he was still afraid. Or maybe he couldn't bear to see the innocent Son of God tortured and crucified in this brutal manner. We are not told.

I cannot imagine the agony and darkness Peter felt over the next days. Crushed. Bewildered. Running all the *I should have* scenarios through his mind. We do know, however, that Peter, unlike Judas, returned to the other disciples. On the first day of the week, Peter was with them when three women showed up and told their story about the empty tomb and the man dressed in a white robe who'd said to them, "Do not be amazed; you are looking for Jesus the Nazarene, who has been crucified. He has risen; He is not here; behold, here is the place where they laid Him. But go, tell His disciples and Peter" (Mark 16:6–7). I try to imagine what went through Peter's heart when he heard, "and Peter." *Peter.* Called out by name. I imagine that a deep thrill of hope rose within him. Could it be true that Jesus had risen? And if so, that his Lord wanted to be sure that he, Peter, was *personally* told?

John 20 tells us that the "disciple whom Jesus loved" and Peter both ran—dare I say *sprinted*—to the tomb. The other disciple stopped outside and peered in, but, of course, impetuous, impatient Peter ran all the way inside the tomb to see for himself and "went away to his home, marveling at what had happened" (Luke 24:12).

How fascinating that both Peter and Judas experienced the same Jesus . . . but their responses were so different.

Judas was protecting his position.

Peter was protecting his life.

In Gethsemane, Judas was a sweet and disarming traitor.

123

In Gethsemane, Peter was a courageous warrior, ready for battle to keep Jesus safe.

Judas had expectations of who Jesus would and should be. He possibly became frustrated and angry when Jesus didn't live up to those expectations.

Peter wanted to know who Jesus truly was, even if the reality didn't meet up with his expectations.

Judas wanted the truth to conform to his expectations.

Peter wanted his expectations to conform to the truth.

Judas listened to himself and the spirit of lies. *Psst. Hey, Judas. Want to be an important guy? Want to set yourself up as powerful?*

Peter listened to the Holy Spirit of truth, even when that truth convicted him of betraying the Son of God.

Judas ran away from Jesus and toward the enemies of Jesus.

Peter ran toward Jesus—he followed Him, sought out Jesus's disciples after the crucifixion, ran toward the tomb, and was with Jesus after His resurrection. He was eager for restoration.

Judas rejected the grace of God.

Peter knew and accepted that grace.

After the resurrection, Jesus fixed breakfast on the beach for the disciples following a long night of fishing (see John 21:12–17). They were sitting around the fire talking, laughing, telling stories, and relaxing when Jesus turned to Peter and asked him, "Simon, son of John, do you love Me (with

124

God-like love) more than these?" Peter answered, "Yes, Lord; you know that I love You (like a brother)." Jesus told him to tend the lambs, the young and weak ones. Again, Jesus asked, "Simon, son of John, do you love Me (with God-like love)?" Peter responded, "Yes, Lord; You know that I love You (like a brother)." Jesus told him to "shepherd My sheep," to be a leader. Then a third time, Jesus changed the word He used for love and asked, "Simon, son of John, do you love Me (like a brother)?" This time Peter was "grieved" that Jesus asked him the same question and responded by saying, "Lord, You know all things; You know I love You (like a brother)." Jesus said to Peter, "Tend My sheep."

Jesus knew Peter needed to affirm, in public, three times— as many times as he'd denied Jesus—his love for Him. When Jesus asked the same question for the third time, I sense in Peter's reply a certain resignation. Peter was honest with himself. He no longer could boast of his love for Jesus. He knew he had failed Jesus. He knew he needed forgiveness and restoration. And so he told Jesus the truth. He couldn't love with God-like love. And Jesus was showing Peter, and the others watching and listening, that Peter, though he was broken by his betrayal of Jesus, was qualified for service for Jesus.

This story demonstrates such an intimate encounter be-tween Peter and Jesus. Peter recognized Jesus knew what he had done but, unlike Judas, his failure didn't cause him to give up. He was deeply sorrowful and repentant. Jesus knew Peter would be a more effective leader as a broken man—no longer headstrong. And the pride he'd had was shattered. So He commissioned Peter to tend His lambs. The weak ones. The ones who needed tenderness and kindness. Peter was capable of that now. If only Judas would have repented to God . . .

Peter knew he could be forgiven. Judas did not. Peter is the one who had asked Jesus how many times they should forgive and heard Jesus say "seventy times seven" for the same offense (Matt. 18:22). Perhaps Peter remembered this and knew Christ could forgive him for three denials (see Matt. 18:31–35).

Will you, like Peter, turn to Jesus when faced with the need for forgiveness? Will you turn to His people? Will you run toward His presence? Will you declare your love and your willingness to serve Jesus in spite of the worst sins you have committed? If so, you, like Peter, will find the open arms of your loving Lord who forgives you completely and restores you to serve Him in ways you cannot imagine.

EIGHT

The Importance
of Community

At the core of every human being is the desire for deep
and satisfying relationships because we are created in
the image of God.

Greg Ogden

As I thought about the stories of Jesus in the Garden of
Gethsemane and Peter after his betrayal of Jesus, I was
surprised to see a common theme I'd never noticed before.
Both Jesus and Peter turned to community when they were
troubled and in need of God's help.

When Jesus went to the garden to pour out His anguish
to His Father in preparation for His sacrifice for our forgiveness, He turned to His community—the disciples—for
support. He took the eleven with Him to the garden, then
narrowed that group down to just Peter, James, and John

to come closer to His place of prayer. We know that all the disciples let Him down by falling asleep. So too will our community—the church—let us down at times. But Jesus, even knowing they would disappoint Him, still took the disciples with Him, desired their support, and gave them the opportunity to support Him. Peter, likewise, returned to his fellow disciples and was with them when the women returned from the tomb. He was also with them a week later when Jesus made them a breakfast of fresh fish.

The Holy Spirit is at work among His people, for it is in the church, the body of Christ, where the gifts of the Spirit are exercised. There is a reason we are not to neglect gathering together with other believers, and I believe that applies to us when we are struggling with forgiveness—either giving it or receiving it or both—just as it applies at other times. Galatians 6:2 tells us, "Bear one another's burdens, and thereby fulfill the law of Christ."

I will be the first to say, however, that doing so is not without risk. Just look at Jesus. On the most critically important night of His life, His closest friends kept falling asleep on Him! The church is made up of broken, leaky vessels, but the light of Christ still shines through the cracks. The Holy Spirit is always at work among His people. Hebrews 13:7 weaves God's help together with the body in a surprising way. "Remember those who led you, who spoke the word of God to you; and considering the result of their conduct, imitate their faith." We are to remember those who led us, who spoke God's Word to us, those whose faith is such that we should imitate it. If it was worth it to Jesus and Peter to risk reaching out for community, then let's imitate them!

Dark Days

When I learned of my first husband's infidelity, my first response was to *comfort* my husband, the one who'd wounded me. I remember telling him it must have been difficult to be having affairs, covering them up as best as he could while carrying on his work in the Christian media business. He had to pretend. I told him I forgave him, and I believed I did. The truth is I was in shock.

I believe that shock is God's protection for us when we can't absorb what has happened. Shock carried me over the first wave of pain. It allowed me time to think and pray. But then I moved into denial and isolation. At first I didn't grasp the importance of staying in fellowship with the body of Christ. I wanted to crawl in a hole. I kept my pain and suffering a secret. I didn't let anyone in—except for my pastor and his wife, who were close friends of both my husband and me. I needed them to help me navigate something so foreign to me. I appreciated their counsel and availability to me. I received no condemnation, only prayerful support. But for everyone else I put on my "everything is fine" mask and pretended it was. I worked hard to look normal on the outside. I believe my isolation thwarted my healing, my growth, and my capacity to forgive.

During that time, one of my daughters was trying to start a chapter of the Fellowship of Christian Athletes in her high school. I agreed to host a gathering of interested folks one Sunday afternoon. My heart ached as the crowd, including my sister Anne and her family, arrived and visited. I slipped away, went to my bedroom, and stepped into my closet to hide for a while. I did not want to face anyone. I may have looked okay, but I wasn't.

Around that time my father turned seventy years old, and my family gathered at Disney World to celebrate. My husband and I acted "normal." But now as I look at the photographs from that celebration I can see the deep pain behind our smiles and in our eyes. No one in the family knew what we were trying to cope with in isolation.

Why didn't we tell our family? My husband was the son of my parents' good friends. They all worked closely together. It was a difficult, complicated situation. I didn't want to hurt any of them, nor did I want to lose face, so I carried the secret that was damaging me. I was uncomfortable with others knowing and yet longed for them to know so I could receive their love and support. But I feared the unsolicited advice I was sure to get. How could they begin to know what my situation was like? How could I begin to tell them?

In my imagination, I thought of many and varied scenarios. All of them were scary. I imagined people blaming me. Telling me what was wrong with me—that I wasn't spiritual enough or I wasn't trusting God enough. I knew I couldn't take that; I was very fragile emotionally.

The longer I held on to the secret, the bigger it got. I used a lot of energy to keep it hidden. But the reality was I couldn't tunnel under it, climb over it, or move around it. I couldn't see my way through. The eyes of my mind were clouded, blinded by the secrecy and the need to keep the secret safe within.

I was reading my Bible and praying, as had been my habit all my life. But where was God? I felt as if heaven's gates were locked from the inside and I was standing outside banging on them. The only sound I heard was the reverberation of my own cries. I felt a horrible loneliness. If only I would have confided in some mature believers, perhaps I would have heard and experienced God's love through them, but I stayed isolated.

Trying to make the abnormal look normal was crazy-making and took its toll. Depression set in. As time progressed, I became very weary. I wasn't sleeping or eating. I could barely function. Getting out of bed was almost more than I could do. Grocery shopping was a Herculean task. The depression became all-consuming. Finally, I began to succumb to thoughts of taking my own life. I began to fantasize about it and planned how I would do it. When you are ill you think so many unhealthy, bizarre things. One Sunday I decided I could take it no longer. I ran from church and went home looking for razor blades. But my husband used an electric razor, so I couldn't find any!

God gave me a moment to think more clearly. He had given me three children to love and protect. They were depending on me. I couldn't, wouldn't, do that to them. I realized I needed help. I decided to go home and tell my mother what was going on. (Daddy wasn't home at the time.) My pastor assured me he would call Mother to tell her I was on my way. I packed some clothes and started the six-hour drive. Tears ran down my cheeks as sobs escaped my heart on that tortuous drive.

The next morning, sitting in the kitchen with our coffee, I told Mother what was going on. She told me she wondered what was wrong, and the rest of the family also sensed that all was not right. I seemed withdrawn and not myself. They had wondered if *I* was having an affair! I thought, as my mother, she would know me better than that. Her mistaken assumption was just one more hurt to bear. She was kind and sympathetic, then suggested I go home, put on a negligee, and make love to my husband. She didn't understand at all. I burst into tears and told her I couldn't do that. I tried to understand where she was coming from and realized she didn't have the tools for this. She wanted to make it right in the only way she knew how.

Now, at least, my mother knew. But she was in frail health and would need someone else—other than me—with whom to talk and ask advice. When I got back to my home in Virginia, shaking from head to toe, I picked up the phone and called my oldest sister's husband, Stephan Tchividjian, at his office. Hearing his voice nearly caused me to break down. I loved him dearly; he was the older brother I never had. He was a clinical psychologist in Florida and a wise, godly man. I told him I had shared something with Mother she would probably need to talk over with him. I didn't want her to carry my burden alone. At that point, I didn't want to tell him my story, but being a wise, godly psychologist, he asked the right questions until I told him. The first thing he said to me was, "We need to get you well. You are not crazy."

Those words brought such comfort. There was hope of healing for me! I wasn't crazy! I had carried all this in secret, thinking it would go away, not wanting to involve others, not wanting to be exposed. One reason is that I blamed myself. *If I was a better wife . . . a better lover . . . more understanding . . . he might not have had the affairs.* Oh, what a dead-end street those thoughts are! Each person is responsible for his or her own choices, and I was in no way responsible for my husband's affairs. Carrying his secret had made me sick—emotionally, physically, and, to some extent, spiritually.

In the process of telling Stephan, I realized God would have to take over. I could no longer handle this situation by myself. Did a sudden clarity come to me? No. Healing is not sudden. But the decision I made to share my secret allowed the Holy Spirit to enter the situation.

I could try to contain and control the flow of information by keeping everything to myself, but I realized now that might abort God's plan for me. That was not trusting God to take care of me. In trying to hold on to the secret to keep myself protected, I had locked Him out by locking His people out. I believe that hindered God's work in my life. Yes, God was digging deep into the soil of my life.

Stepping out of the Shadows

Once Mother and Stephan knew, I could no longer keep the extended family in the dark. At first I hoped that when the others knew what I was enduring, they would think me so strong and brave and spiritual! Mother used to say, "It's not so difficult to suffer in silence as long as everybody knows you're doing it." That's where I was, but my thinking was totally unrealistic and unhelpful.

After I was no longer keeping our struggle a secret, word spread to a larger circle. There were those I expected to understand or support me who didn't. They talked *to* me and *at* me, but their advice was without empathy. Many dished out platitudes. They seemed to have their own agendas and could not hear my heart's cry. Some saw my anger as rebellion, not as a natural, normal, and appropriate reaction to a deep wound. Sadly, this is when I first experienced how the church can sometimes shoot its wounded. (Actually, "bury its wounded" would be more accurate. Shooting would have been more merciful!)

At this point you may be wondering, given this experience, why I recommend that we turn to the body of Christ. I'm not suggesting that you shout your personal problems from the rooftops, but I am suggesting that you seek out a few wise, mature, and trusted confidants who will listen, support, encourage, and pray for you as you learn how to give and receive forgiveness.

I found a wise counselor who could lead me through a period of discovery and healing from a biblical worldview. What a huge difference it made! At first I had to reject the thinking that needing a counselor meant I was spiritually deficient or that my faith wasn't strong enough. It didn't take long for me to realize I needed to be open with the counselor about what was happening in my life. It was scary. But I felt wholeness was waiting on the other side, and I was desperate to be whole. I got to the point that it didn't matter what others thought—I wanted to be free.

Being in community is essential to our well-being. It is not an option. From the very beginning, God said it is not good to be alone. He gave Adam Eve. He built family. Then He instituted the church for His children to come together to share life. Jesus Himself traveled with twelve men—doing life and ministry together.

The apostle John wrote, "What we have seen and heard we proclaim to you also, so that you too may have fellowship with us; and indeed our fellowship is with the Father, and with His Son Jesus Christ" (1 John 1:3). There is fellowship in community. Fellowship has to do with belonging, companionship. A sense of belonging is one of the deep needs of the human spirit. And we are invited into fellowship with God Himself and His Son, Jesus.

There is purpose to being in community. The writer of Hebrews wrote, "And let us consider how to stimulate one another to love and good deeds, not forsaking our own assembling together" (10:24–25). Being in community stimulates us to love more, care more, and act in compassionate ways. It is a source of encouragement and challenge to be all God wants us to be. It keeps us from being self-centered. Being in community is the means by which God has ordained we grow in our spiritual life.

I am an introvert. I recharge my energy by being alone. It's easier for me to be alone. But I find if I stay in my aloneness, my thinking becomes circular—there is no one to interact with my thinking or challenge me to look at something differently. My perspective narrows. I need those who will come alongside to stimulate my thinking and help me broaden my perspective—all with the Bible as the filter.

This community must be a safe place. It must be an honest place and a place of encouragement. A place of mutual vulnerability. A place where confidences can be shared and kept secure. In such an environment, forgiveness can flourish.

In recent years I have made the deliberate choice to widen my community because I have realized I need it for my continued spiritual growth—we all do. There are no exceptions. I have found this community in church, faithful friends, and Bible study.

I have a friend whom I'll call Jill. As a child, she had been sexually molested by a cousin. Years later, as an adult believer, Jill declared she would never forgive her cousin. Then, through the body of Christ, Jill had two experiences.

First, she read the book *One Light Still Shines* by a believer, Marie Monville. Marie was the wife of the man who invaded an Amish schoolhouse and shot ten girls before turning the gun on himself and committing suicide. Jill wrote to me,

> *To see how the Amish chose to forgive immediately and not only that but protect the wife from the media during her husband's funeral was such a convicting message to me. I realized that I wanted to wait for the hurt feelings to fade to forgive. I now understand that forgiving is a choice and God will help me with the feelings.*

Secondly, Jill attended some meetings at a local church led by an organization called G.R.A.C.E., Godly Response to Abuse in a Christian Environment. She wrote,

> *I found that each time I participated in G.R.A.C.E. training . . . there was more healing. Hearing Christians show concern instead of denial toward sexual abuse was one of the main factors. The acknowledgment that the training and meetings were stressful and that we should take care of ourselves helped. The teaching on the biblical perspective of protecting the sheep was so rich. . . . Having research, facts, and truth helped. In particular, he shared that it is not true that most perpetrators had been molested as a child. For me that took away the fear that people might wonder about me if I shared that I had been molested. Being able to look at a case study and discuss it was a real learning*

experience. Just being able to speak of the "unspeak-able" and know that it was okay and I was believed helped me.

Jill's journey through forgiveness was supported and enhanced by the body of Christ. What an inspiring example of the church being the church in the very best sense!

From Conflict to Unity

Peter and Paul serve as examples through their writings of how the church can be the best of itself. Interestingly, they also give us an example of discord and disagreement in the body. As one who has been wounded by fellow believers and who has wounded fellow believers, I appreciate this example. It shows that even well-meaning and committed believers can clash yet can also work through their conflict to eventual forgiveness and unity.

Paul was a highly educated rabbi and a talented debater. By trade, he was a skilled tentmaker. While in Corinth he worked with Priscilla and Aquila to make a living.

Peter was an uneducated fisherman. Big. Burly. Tough. Rough hands and rough personality. He tended to be impulsive and mercurial—seeming at times to be volatile and unpredictable.

Both were leaders and both loved God.

In spite of Peter's denial the night Jesus was betrayed, Jesus commissioned Peter to be the rock of the church.

In spite of Paul's part in killing Christians (as Saul), Jesus commissioned Paul to take the message of the gospel to everyone—including the Gentiles.

Both were examples of God choosing broken people to serve Him. Both longed to honor and serve Christ, promoting the gospel wherever they could.

One day, Peter went up to a rooftop to pray but was distracted by his hunger and wanted to eat. (Can you relate?) Scripture says he saw a vision of a sheet lowered from the sky filled with animals and birds and crawling creatures. The voice of God commanded him to kill and eat. Peter said, "Whoa. Wait a minute, God. I have never eaten anything unholy or unclean." The response came: "What God has cleansed, no longer consider unholy" (Acts 10:15). This happened three times. (Since "threes" are a common theme in Peter's life, it seems as though he needed to have things repeated so they could find a permanent place in his brain.)

From that point on, Peter promoted unity among believers, whether Jew or Gentile, providing a living example for others by eating with Gentile believers—something that had not been done in the past. There had always been a risk of eating something forbidden by the law or contaminated by idol worship. Yet now Peter led the way as the last barrier between Jews and Gentiles—dietary restrictions—was abolished. Can you imagine how this must have felt to the Gentiles, who were formerly marginalized for what they ate? They went from being different and left out to being wholeheartedly accepted into the family of God. This acceptance came not only from a Jew but from an apostle of Jesus himself!

During the Council at Jerusalem (a conference of Christian elders and leaders), Peter preached on the subject of lifting dietary restrictions to the elders, challenging them to see the Gentile believers as their equals. There is no distinction in Christ. All believers belong to the family of God as equals. Many followed his example, trusting Peter as their leader. Yet after he preached those words of challenge, a different group of Jews came to town. When they arrived, everything changed. We don't know why, but Peter may have been intimidated by these men. He withdrew from the Gentiles, "held himself aloof," and began to eat according to the stricter rules of Jewish law that had been abolished. Oh, how that must have hurt and confused those new Gentile believers! They were now, again, treated like second-class citizens in their newfound family. Peter was ignoring the clear revelation from God to make no distinction between circumcised and uncircumcised, Jew and Gentile. To eat freely of all food. His leadership was so powerful that "the rest of the Jews joined him in hypocrisy" (Gal. 2:13).

This angered Paul. How could Peter and the others talk about the unity of all believers while holding a double standard? Paul refused to stand by and watch as Peter and those following him were not only stepping away from God's clear revelation but also making obedience to the law once again the criteria for salvation. Paul was all about the cross, and he wasn't going to let this fundamental issue go unaddressed. He stood up to Peter in front of everyone and chastised him, even though cultural custom dictated that you confront someone in private. This was embarrassing!

I can only imagine the confrontation. Harsh words were spoken. Voices were raised. Paul would not back down, and Peter struggled to admit Paul was right. After all, Paul was the last to "come to the party." How could he speak so authoritatively? He hadn't even been a disciple of Jesus. This did not sit well with Peter.

Perhaps the others tried to mediate the argument. No doubt lines were drawn and sides taken, threatening to divide the infant church. It was serious. We know Barnabas sided with Peter. We are not told in Scripture what happened, but Paul, in Galatians 2, wrote what he said to Peter in Antioch. It was direct. It was firm. It was uncompromising.

The sad result was that there was a rift in relationships. For a time, Peter and Paul went their separate ways.

No doubt Peter was hurt by Paul but also by his own poor choices that hurt others. Yet, somewhere along the way, there was a restoration of forgiveness and unity. It is evident that Peter forgave Paul for rebuking him in public and accepted his words of rebuke, referring to Paul in 2 Peter 3:15 as "our beloved brother." From their writings, we know Peter and Paul agreed on the doctrine of grace—that we are saved by grace, not works. These men eventually moved forward, harmoniously, by the grace of God and His Spirit.

When Paul wrote, "Be angry and yet do not sin" in Ephesians 4:26, was he thinking of his disagreement with Peter? And then he went on to write,

> Do not grieve the Holy Spirit of God, by whom you were sealed for the day of redemption. Let all bitterness and wrath and anger and clamor and slander be put away from you, along with all malice. Be kind to one another, tender-hearted, forgiving each other, just as God in Christ also has forgiven you. (vv. 30–32)

I would venture to say that this is how they settled their disagreement. It is a pattern for us to follow.

I like the way *The Message* puts Ephesians 4:30–32:

Don't grieve God. Don't break his heart. His Holy Spirit, moving and breathing in you, is the most intimate part of your life, making you fit for himself. Don't take such a gift for granted.

Make a clean break with all cutting, backbiting, profane talk. Be gentle with one another, sensitive. Forgive one another as quickly and thoroughly as God in Christ forgave you.

Clearly, the unity of community is critically important. Forgiveness is the pathway to restoring and keeping that unity. Jesus knew we would face challenges with one another. In John 17:11, in the midst of Jesus praying for His followers, listen to the prayer He prayed for us. He prayed that we would live in unity. "Keep them in Your name, the name which You have given Me, that they may be one even as We are."

Through forgiveness, may we too be one. May we, like Jill, turn to the body of Christ for help and resources to work through our pain to find forgiveness.

May you, like me, discover that by breaking our silence and turning to godly believers we are able to find in community a safe place where encouragement, mutual vulnerability, and secure confidences can be found so that we can grow spiritually.

May we, like Jesus and Peter, turn to community when we are troubled and in need of God's help.

NINE

Blessings Not Bitterness

Bitterness keeps your pain alive instead of letting you deal with it and get beyond it. Bitterness sentences you to relive the hurt over and over.

Lee Strobel

One afternoon the phone rang. I picked it up and heard "her" voice. Instantly, I felt knots in my stomach. I pretended to be glad to hear from her while my familiar internal script scrolled through my mind. *She is so patronizing and controlling. I've tried, but I can hardly bear to interact with her. If she tells me one more time . . .*

Did anyone come to your mind as you read that? Some person in your life whom the mere mention of sets your stomach to churning or the sound of whose voice sends your blood pressure rising? I'd love to say that I made up that scenario, but sadly it is true. She had wounded me many times. Where once I'd felt only irritation, over time my emotions toward this person had grown to bitterness, and I knew it.

When someone has wounded us deeply or repeatedly, it is natural, it is human, to become bitter. The relationship is unfair and lopsided. The person seems to walk away after an encounter with nary a bruise while you are on the ground slashed and bleeding. Have you noticed that the bitterness just adds to the agony? As in my scenario above, "she" didn't suffer from my bitterness, I did! As Lee Strobel expressed, bitterness sentences us to relive our hurt over and over.

Emotions come unbidden. We will feel all sorts of emotions, whether we want to or not. At times we will feel bitter. That's normal. We don't have to feel guilty about it. But we don't have to set up camp and live there either. Hebrews 12:15 tells us, "See to it that no one comes short of the grace of God; that no root of bitterness springing up causes trouble, and by it many be defiled." For bitterness to take root, it has to be given time to germinate. And we have to nurture it, water it, and fertilize it for the roots to go down deep into our heart and soul. When that happens, it affects not only us but those around us.

How many times did I say snide things about my children's father because of the bitterness I harbored? How much damage did it do to their relationship? I had not let God do His transforming work in my spirit. Still angry, I was too busy justifying myself. Yes, I had reason to be angry. But God wasn't going to let me get away with bitterness. He loved me too much. And the same was true of my bitterness toward the woman on the phone. Satan, the enemy, was gaining ground in my life as the bitterness invaded my soul.

Have you ever tasted a cup of really dark, bitter coffee? Or unsweetened cocoa powder? Neither tastes good, and it's hard to get rid of the disagreeable flavor in your mouth. Bitterness is like that, only it resides deep within.

Bitterness is something we are very familiar with. We have seen it in others, have felt it ourselves, and perhaps have acted on it. We talk about something being "a bitter pill to swallow." But what does the word *bitterness* mean? Among other definitions, my dictionary uses the words *resentful, cynicism,* and *rancor.* The thesaurus uses words like *acrimony, animosity,* and *hostile* among other nasty words. The Bible uses the word to describe speech such as angry words, hard labor as in servitude, or the misery of rebelling against God. It describes a life of sin as being bitter.[1] An injustice is bitter. Regret is bitter. When one is bitter, he or she easily takes offense. It is not pleasant for them or for those around them. Why would anyone want to hang on to their bitterness? I suppose because it fuels our anger and gives us a sense of power.

Bitterness may start as just a little hurt feeling. But as we return to those thoughts time and again, reviewing and reliving the hurt, we are nurturing that tiny seed. We talk to our friends about the event. We get them to assume our perspective, thereby tainting them with our bitterness. The roots dig yet deeper. If we don't conquer it, it will conquer us.

The book of Genesis tells the story of two brothers. Their rivalry is infamous, and bitterness plays a key role in their relationship.

Jacob and Esau

Sibling rivalry has always been with us. But as far as I know, the only reference to sibling rivalry beginning in the womb is that of Jacob and Esau.

These boys, the grandsons of Abraham and Sarah, were born later in life to Rebekah and Isaac after years of Rebekah's barrenness. What a heritage these twins had: a great patriarch and a great matriarch in their ancestry!

The Bible tells us that things started off badly. Rebekah felt the babies struggle within her and wondered what was happening. She'd never been pregnant, so she didn't know and went to the One who would know—God. God explained to her that her babies represented two nations, two peoples, and one would be stronger than the other. He told her the older would serve the younger, which was not the norm in their culture. It was custom for the oldest male child to be the heir, take leadership, and become the head of the family.

Rebekah's fraternal twins were unalike from birth, complete opposites of each other; the elder, named Esau, was hairy all over and became a "skillful hunter, a man of the field" (Gen. 25:27), loving the outdoors. The younger, Jacob, was born holding the heel of his brother as he emerged from his mother's womb. He "was a peaceful man, living in tents" (v. 27). It was likely that this son learned all the business-type aspects of taking care of this large group of people that included family and many servants. "Living in tents" probably means he was a shepherd as well, tending the flocks of sheep and goats necessary for the family's survival.

Esau was a child who always wanted to be out roughhousing and charging about. The captain-of-the-football-team type. Jacob was a child who preferred quietness and plainness. He chose to become a shepherd—the kind of work where someone who favors solitude and quiet would thrive. Such differences are often seen in families. However, when you add favoritism, as happened in this family, you have an explosive situation of competition and sibling rivalry. In this case, Isaac preferred Esau—perhaps because he was a man's man—and Rebekah preferred Jacob—perhaps because she remembered that the Lord had told her that the older would serve the younger.

One day Esau was out in the field, working hard. He was very tired and hungry. On his way home, he saw Jacob making a stew. This was his family recipe. He asked Jacob for some of the stew because he was ravenous. Jacob, being a clever fellow, wanted to take advantage of the situation and told Esau he would exchange a bowl of stew for Esau's birthright, which included the inheritance. Esau rashly agreed— even made an oath to that effect. He reasoned the birthright would be of no use to him if he died of hunger. Esau satisfied his hunger and went on his way. Perhaps both Esau and Jacob thought they had gotten away with something—that they had outwitted each other.

In that culture and time, the birthright was what every firstborn son anticipated. Through it they received not only a double portion of the estate but also the lineage that would carry the family name. In this case, as the descendants of Abraham, the inheritance involved far more than just the money, livestock, lands, or possessions that most sons would receive. The one who had the extra portion would also carry on the bloodline through whom God had promised the Messiah.

> By selling his birthright for a bowl of stew, Esau overtly expressed his contempt for God, for that birthright included the covenant promise which God made to Abraham, to be passed on to and through his family line. Esau's act showed how little he valued God or his promises.[2]

Esau *despised* his birthright. He didn't just sell it, he had only contempt for it. It meant less than nothing to him.

Years passed. Isaac grew old and nearly blind. One day he was hungry for a certain kind of dish Esau made from the game he killed. He called for Esau and told him to go out and hunt, make the dish, and bring it to him, at which time Isaac would bless Esau with the family blessing, establishing Esau as Isaac's heir. He would have the birthright. Isaac didn't know Esau had sold it to Jacob years before, and Esau didn't volunteer to tell him the truth.

Rebekah overheard the conversation and, perhaps remembering God's promise that Jacob was to rule over the older son, hatched her own plan. She told Jacob to bring her two young goats so she could make the stew Isaac enjoyed. Jacob would take the stew to his father and pretend to be Esau. After Isaac ate the stew, Jacob would receive the blessing in Esau's place. Jacob may have rolled his eyes and told her the plan wouldn't work because even though Isaac couldn't see, he would feel Jacob's smooth skin, a clear contrast to hairy Esau. But Rebekah had already thought of a solution for that. She got some of Esau's clothes, which smelled like him, and had goatskins to cover Jacob's hands and neck so they would feel hairy. After preparing Jacob to pass for Esau, she gave him bread and the stew.

Jacob then went to his father and offered him the food. He encouraged his father to eat, then to bless him.

Isaac sensed something was not quite right. It hadn't taken enough time for the young man to hunt the animals and then make the dish. He asked Jacob if he was really Esau. Jacob lied and assured his father he was Esau. He even used God, saying God had given him success in the hunt. Still his father wasn't convinced. He knew the voice was Jacob's, and yet the hands felt like Esau's. Isaac asked him again if he was Esau. Jacob lied a second time, assuring him he was.

After Isaac finished eating, he told Jacob to come close so he could bless him. As Jacob drew near, his father kissed him. Because Jacob's clothes smelled like Esau, Isaac was reassured that this was the correct son and blessed him with the patriarchal blessing. Jacob then stood, the rightful heir of not only the double portion of the firstborn son but also the holy covenant. It could not be undone.

What followed was like a scene in a theatrical play. After Jacob exited stage left with an empty bowl and a full blessing, Esau entered stage right bearing his own prepared dish of steaming stew. "My father, please sit up and eat some of my game, so that you may give me your blessing" (Gen. 27:31 NIV).

The scene played out exactly as before. The father asked who approached. The son claimed to be Esau. After a moment of confusion, Isaac realized the truth and told Esau the blessing was gone.

The Bible says, "When Esau heard his father's words, he burst out with a loud and bitter cry and said to his father, 'Bless me—me too, my father!'" (v. 34 NIV).

Following his outcry, Esau growled that Jacob had been correctly named because he was a deceiver. Not only had he taken Esau's birthright but also his blessing.

Isn't it interesting how Esau distorted the facts? Jacob hadn't *taken* Esau's birthright, Esau had eagerly *sold* it for a pot of stew. When had Esau twisted these facts in his mind? Had he lived for many years in self-deceit, not telling himself the truth but building a different story in his mind? Or did he, in this moment of accountability, conveniently blame Jacob for his long-ago choice? Don't we do the same? We don't like taking responsibility for our part. We distort the truth.

When Isaac told Esau that he had made Jacob master over him and all his brothers, plus giving him the elder son's portion of material goods, Esau was beside himself, begging for a blessing as well. Isaac finally gave him the "leftover" blessing.

The Bible says Esau held a grudge against Jacob because of the blessing his father had given him. He said to himself, "The days of mourning for my father are near; then I will kill my brother Jacob" (v. 41 NIV).

Someone reported Esau's threat to Rebekah. She went to Jacob to tell him to flee to her brother, Laban, and stay for a few days until Esau's fury subsides and "[he] forgets what you did to him" (v. 45). (Interesting that she seems to not include herself in the scheme she initiated! We rewrite our own history.) Jacob fled immediately to Haran. Little did he know he would be gone from home not just a few days but twenty years—and would never see his mother again.

Jacob's new life did not prove to be easy. He fell in love with Laban's daughter Rachel and agreed to work for seven years to earn her hand in marriage. On the wedding night Laban substituted Leah, Rachel's older sister. Jacob was not happy that he had been tricked. He felt the full brunt of what it was like to be completely deceived. Perhaps now he understood his brother's fury. He confronted Laban. Laban gave Rachel to him as a wife too but told Jacob he had to work another seven years for her.

If we look closely, we see evidence of God's grace in the midst of the bitterness between the brothers. Later in Scripture we see that Jacob is no longer only conniving and manipulative but has become humble. Esau did not kill his brother as he had vowed to do. Surely he could have sought Jacob out and taken his life, but he didn't. Years later, when they crossed paths, we see an Esau who is no longer angry and bitter nor vengeful. God had done a work in them.

We are not given the specifics, but perhaps they had matured not only as men but as men of God. They were now able to give to each other honor and dignity and deference. They had spent years apart and gained the time and perspective to see God's hand in their lives. They no longer were leaning on their own understanding but trusting God. It's really a lovely ending to what started as a terrible story of brotherhood gone wrong. They did not live together—they went their separate ways, but with each other's blessing.

Let's take a look at the choices we have when we taste bitterness in our own hearts.

Marie's Choices

I had a friend who has now gone to be with the Lord. Her father, like mine, was an evangelist. We had a lot in common. As a young girl, she said goodbye to her father and mother too many times as they traveled for months at a time. Little "Marie" was left in the care of her grandmother over and over again. She missed her parents. She cried when they left town. She was an only child and would get so lonely staying with her grandmother.

As often happens in families steeped in ministry, she was told her parents were out serving the Lord and she shouldn't complain. But she resented all the times her parents left her.

She was unhappy. She learned to cover it and keep the Christian image she thought she was supposed to portray, but beneath the surface bitterness took root. Marie went on to college and eventually married.

Her husband became successful in his business. It all looked good on the outside, but Marie still held on to the bitterness of being left so often when she was young. There were moments of anger that flared in their home, but there was no talk of conflict resolution or forgiveness. Instead she just covered over her resentment with Bible verses and "moved on" in a way that looked like forgiveness. Marie would talk about her heartache of being left alone as a little girl and even incorporated it into her testimony. It was a good story, and it sounded as if she'd dealt with it in a healthy way.

Over time Marie had four children. She began to speak regularly and teach Bible classes. She was admired by many. Her husband frequently traveled for business, and her schedule also took her away from home. Can you surmise how she cared for her children under those circumstances? She often left them in the care of her parents! Yes, she repeated the same pattern she had resented as a child.

The years passed and her children each went off to college, married, and established Christian homes, all nearby. But Marie's bitterness had become a lifelong presence in her life, often expressed in controlling behavior, and was never far from the surface. No one would have called Marie warm—some described her as an icicle—but she did her best to play the part of warm Bible teacher, mother, and family matriarch.

One of her sons married a young woman, "Lisa," and the marriage looked ideal from the outside. She was pretty and he was handsome. Marie tried to control Lisa, but she was independent and liked it that way. Lisa also tried to keep up the image of how a Christian woman should look. Hers was not a happy marriage, but she was determined to make it work. What option did she have? Marriage was for life.

Anger soon surfaced in the young couple's marriage. Christian practices became surface and for show, to keep up the image. It saddened me to watch my friend's children struggle.

One day Marie called to tell me her handsome son had had multiple affairs. She was distraught. Nothing had prepared her for this. Her daughter-in-law sought counseling. Her son went to one counseling session with his wife but then declared it wasn't his problem. Marie, concerned, went to visit them and tried to talk to them. She put pressure on Lisa to forgive and move on. Lisa, however, believed her heart and trust were broken beyond fixing, in spite of the fact that the couple had children. This frustrated Marie. She became angry with Lisa. Why wouldn't she keep up the image that all was well? An image that was very important to Marie.

In spite of Marie's anger at Lisa, she kept up the pretense. Ever the image-keeper, she invited Lisa over for dinner and included her on different special occasions. Even after Lisa divorced her son, Marie never indicated she had anger toward her. Lisa was under the impression that the two shared an honest and solid relationship—a relationship that went on for years, until Marie's death.

Then came the shock. At the reading of Marie's will, her hidden bitterness came to light. Where once the children had been told the will included some money to Lisa's children, now it did not. Her bitterness bore fruit—now her grandchildren were stung with the fact that they were not treated equally in the will. As I watched this unfold, I grieved over the painful legacy Marie left for those grandchildren, and I contrasted it to the legacy of joy and godliness my own mother left for my children.

Bitterness always bears fruit. It may take years to reveal itself. But it will. As Hebrews 12:15 warns, bitterness can grow a root that, when it springs up, will cause trouble, and many will be defiled by it. In other words, bitterness doesn't just affect us. If left to grow in our hearts and minds, it will not only poison our own souls but will affect others.

If you and I harbor bitterness and keep nursing anger over the wrong done to us, we are allowing the roots to dig deep into our spirit. That's not a place I want to be—where dark things live! I want a light, loving, gentle spirit. A loving spirit cannot dwell with a bitter one.

How to Tell If You've Forgiven or Not

I sometimes wonder if my friend Marie was even aware of the degree of bitterness she felt toward her own parents and toward Lisa. Perhaps her efforts of image-keeping were really misguided attempts to overcome her negative emotions. Who knows? Self-deception can have a powerful pull on us.

We have to go back to chapter 6 and review the choices we have when we are wounded: choosing confession, choosing to be brave enough to ask forgiveness and grant it, choosing to be a forgiving person, and choosing to discern if reconciliation is in order. If only Marie would have made those choices. If we are not making those choices for ourselves, then the likelihood of our anger turning into bitterness increases. Let's agree that forgiveness takes courage and, as we discussed in chapter 7, we must be willing to ask for help from the Holy Spirit. It is foolhardy to think we can accomplish this impossible task under our own power.

How do we keep moving forward so that our anger doesn't stagnate, left to take root and sprout into bitterness? *We must recognize when we haven't yet forgiven.*

One of the ways we can know that we haven't forgiven is when we find ourselves reviewing the wrong over and over, beyond what is necessary for healing. Rehashing the events in your mind is the perfect fertilizer for bitterness.

Also, sharing the wrong with others for any purpose beyond getting help for healing simply reignites the flame of bitterness and brings down the person who wronged you in the eyes of others.

When we are unable to genuinely want the best for the person who wronged us, we need to check where we are in the process of forgiveness. For when we have forgiven, we don't want harm to come to them. We want God's best for them. Even if the situation requires justice in a court of law, we can desire the ultimate best for them: salvation through Jesus.

Another telltale sign our forgiveness is not complete is if we are unwilling to pray blessing over them. As it says in 1 Peter 3:9–11,

> Do not repay evil with evil or insult with insult. On the contrary, repay evil with blessing, because to this you were called so that you may inherit a blessing.
>
> For,
>
> > "Whoever would love life
> > and see good days

must keep their tongue from evil
  and their lips from deceitful speech.
They must turn from evil and do good;
  they must seek peace and pursue it." (NIV)

When we are growing in our forgiveness, we are willing to pray a blessing, even if at first it is through clenched teeth. But you do it in obedience. "Lord, bless Lisa. Pour out Your presence and power into her life and bring the fruit of the Spirit pouring into her life." Can you imagine praying a blessing upon the person who wounded you? Sound impossible? Not with God. Ask for the Holy Spirit's help and just do it every time the person comes to mind. You may need to begin with just a quick "arrow" prayer: "Lord, bless Lisa today."

Here's another test for unforgiveness in your heart. Ask yourself what the first thing is that you think about when you see that person or hear their voice or even hear mention of their name. Is your first thought what that person did to wrong you? Are you critical every time you think of them or are in their presence? Consider these to be red flags that you may have more forgiveness work to do!

Are you able to see the situation through their eyes—perhaps to see that they are broken or flawed, in need of healing and grace—or are you only able to see the situation through the lens of your own pain?

Do you have a hard time being around that person? That may be a red flag as well. Of course, in cases like abuse it would be totally understandable to find it difficult to be around that person—and not wise. Also, a toxic person is someone you may have a hard time being around, for good reason.

Do not hear me saying that these questions apply equally to all circumstances. Certainly, it would not be wise for the abused, the victim, to be around the abuser. Nor can we or should we see the situation through the eyes of those who have performed despicable acts of great harm. For them, the test of whether or not we've forgiven might be, Do I want to see Christ forgive them? Do I want them to find salvation in Christ and be a recipient of grace, bound for eternity in heaven? (This is what the missionary in chapter 1 was able to do.) Or do I want them to rot in hell? These questions are, however, very appropriate for most situations of forgiveness—even for deep betrayals such as I experienced with my first husband.

If you recognize any of the above symptoms in yourself, then it is possible that your process of forgiveness has stalled and bitterness is trying to dig its roots into your heart. But there's hope! God not only equips us with the Holy Spirit when we call on Him for help but His Word equips us with the weapons and strategy we need to fight the battle against bitterness.

Taking Captives

If you are beginning to feel battle weary at the thought of this struggle against bitterness, that may be because you are catching on to the fact that this issue of forgiveness is not simply a matter of psychological well-being and personal growth. To engage in forgiveness is to engage in an all-out battle! Remember what we learned in chapter 2: forgiveness is holy. There is a cosmic battle being fought for the souls on this earth. And though the enemy was defeated at the cross, he is still determined to wound and weaken as many of God's people as he can. He knows that unforgiveness and bitterness can cripple us and render us weak and susceptible to his other schemes. It keeps us living in defeat rather than thriving in the abundant life God promises us.

As it says in Ephesians 6:12, "For our struggle is not against flesh and blood, but against the rulers, against the powers, against the world forces of this darkness, against the spiritual forces of wickedness in the heavenly places."

God provides us with His weapons and strategies. In 2 Corinthians 10:4–5, we read:

> The weapons we fight with are not the weapons of the world. On the contrary, they have divine power to demolish strongholds. We demolish arguments and every pretension that sets itself up against the knowledge of God, and we take captive every thought to make it obedient to Christ. (NIV)

Wow! There are powerful words in those verses—*weapons* with *divine power* to *demolish strongholds.* That's what I want to do to my bitterness. I want to demolish it! And we are given the battle strategy: we are to *take captive every thought and make it obedient to Christ.* And that, I have discovered through personal experience, is not only possible in Christ but is powerful at defeating bitterness. For bitterness begins and lives in our thoughts.

How, precisely, do we take every thought captive?

Slowly. Because it won't come easily. You have to fight for it. You really do have to capture those thoughts by saying, as they come into your mind, "I'm not going there." It takes mental and emotional discipline because it's easy to slide back and entertain such thoughts as rehearsing the wrongs, imagining yourself telling off the one who wronged you, or getting revenge. But we just have to capture those thoughts and immediately say, "Holy Spirit, help me here." You have to do it consciously, which is hard work. But it can be done. It takes practice, but the more you practice, the easier it will come.

Once you have identified the bitter or vengeful or un-Christlike thoughts, you then have to confront them with God's thoughts. This is done by "renewing your mind" with the Word of God.

> And do not be conformed to this world, but be transformed by the renewing of your mind, so that you may prove what the will of God is, that which is good and acceptable and perfect. (Rom. 12:2)

Like forgiveness, taking our thoughts captive and renewing our mind is usually not a one-time event. But sometimes it just may be. I experienced that once when a close friend said some ugly things about me and it got back to me. I was deeply hurt and didn't understand why she had said what she did. I chose to forgive her and asked God to help me "take captive" the emotions and thoughts. I identified each destructive thought that passed into my mind and "renewed my mind" by praying blessings upon her and quoting Scriptures of love and unity. Several months went by, and she came back into town. I knew our paths would cross. I continued praying God would help me, and I grew more fervent in my prayers. The day arrived when I would see her, and I was very anxious. But when I saw my friend, my heart flooded with love and forgiveness that continues to this day. I'd never experienced such an immediate turnaround before! Now I don't even remember what it was she said about me. It's not important. Instead, when I think of her, all I remember is the love and respect we have for each other.

More often than not, I don't experience such a quick and complete turnaround. Usually for me it is more like the Colorado River forming the Grand Canyon—day by day by day, a layer of anger or resentment is removed. Oftentimes it is minute by minute by minute. I have to capture each negative thought and take it to Jesus. I have to consciously stop each negative replay of what happened. I must renew my mind with the truth of what God says about the person, the situation, and me. It's hard work, but bit by bit, little by little, one day I realize I am free.

Even then, it is not uncommon that, one day while I am doing something totally unrelated, the event will wash over me, unbidden. I feel the ugly emotions all over again. It's unexpected and takes me off guard. Satan loves the surprise attack. I try not to get wound up in all the tentacles of the emotions that could tie me up in knots and make me lose the ground I worked so hard to gain. I have to stop right in the moment and remind myself of the decision I made and begin again to renew my mind with God's truth.

As I wrote this chapter, I decided to consult with my nephew, who was an Army Ranger. He understands what battles are all about. He has faced combat in Iraq and Afghanistan. He was awarded the Purple Heart and has taken captives on the battlefield. First, he explained, you must always be on your guard and remain vigilant. He also acknowledged that it is hard not to respond with revenge when your fellow soldiers are killed and wounded. You have to step back, remove yourself from that emotion, and see the situation objectively. "You take ownership of the captives," he explained, "so you have to set conditions to best care for your captives. Think through what will be done with them." Finally, he said, "You have to have a plan for every night, well-planned and well-rehearsed, and you have to reevaluate your plan regularly." Every one of those steps applies perfectly to our taking every thought captive!

Capture such thoughts as bitterness, anger, slander, malice, selfishness, pride, victimhood, blame, revenge, hurt, and shame. Renew your mind with words and verses of grace, mercy, truth, faith, openness, kindness, love, and the memory of God's forgiveness of you. Practice praying a blessing over the person.

Is it hard work? Yes. But it is also worth the effort. Otherwise I let Satan win. But when I use God's weapons and strategy, he cannot take that ground; it belongs to God!

Celebrating Each Victory

Let's revisit the story of the woman on the phone at the opening of this chapter. I recognized my bitterness, and so I asked God to show me a Scripture I could place in my mind to help me forgive her. The Lord led me to Ephesians 4:31–32, and I realized that was the passage I needed. I know we discussed this passage earlier, so let's look at it this time in the New Living Translation: "Get rid of all bitterness, rage, anger, harsh words, and slander, as well as all types of evil behavior. Instead, be kind to each other, tenderhearted, forgiving one another, just as God through Christ has forgiven you."

I memorized it. And each time the phone rang and that woman was on the other end, I would repeat the verses in my mind. Oh, at first it was through gritted teeth! But each time she called it got better until, finally, my battle with bitterness toward her was won. I find that now, rather than wishing I could avoid her, I want to be a blessing in her life.

I celebrate that victory and encourage you to celebrate your victories as well, for remembering what the Lord has done in us and through us builds our faith and reminds us that the battle is the Lord's.

TEN

Telling Yourself the Truth

Tackle your misbeliefs; replace them with the truth.

William Backus and Marie Chapian

Can you think of a person who nearly always finds it particularly hard to forgive you? If you are anything like me, the answer to that question is, "Yes! Me!" How can we forgive ourselves—especially when we are "repeat offenders"?

Have you ever had an experience where you blew it, then made the same mistake or committed the same sin again? Maybe you even knew better but did it anyway. Over the next two chapters, we will explore the connection between forgiving ourselves and forgiving other people in our lives.

Why do we repeat the same mistakes? Why do we try to do what is right but fail over and over again? The apostle Paul asked that same question in Romans 7.

I am all too human, a slave to sin. I don't really understand myself, for I want to do what is right, but I don't do it. Instead, I do what I hate. . . . I want to do what is right, but I can't. I want to do what is good, but I don't. I don't want to do what is wrong, but I do it anyway. . . . I have discovered this principle of life—that when I want to do what is right, I inevitably do what is wrong. I love God's law with all my heart. But there is another power within me that is at war with my mind. This power makes me a slave to the sin that is still within me. Oh, what a miserable person I am! Who will free me from this life that is dominated by sin and death? (vv. 14–15, 18–19, 21–24 NLT)

He seems to express my own frustrations and, no doubt, your own.

Paul then answered his own question in the next two verses. "Thank God! The answer is in Jesus Christ our Lord. . . . So now there is no condemnation for those who belong to Christ Jesus" (7:25–8:1 NLT). My problem is that I know these verses but still struggle to internalize their truth. How about you?

After several years of leading Ruth Graham & Friends as a single woman, I found myself in a deepening friendship with a man I had known for over twenty years. At one point, he'd been a respected pastor and counselor. Then he'd fallen into sin and found himself in trouble with the law. He'd had to serve jail time. His marriage ended. He lost his pastorate, his church, his family, and nearly all his friends. My heart went out to him. He was seemingly penitent and was trying to rebuild his life. He'd submitted himself to some fine, respected men in the community who were elders in their church.

I came alongside him in friendship, wanting very much to live out the grace that I had experienced and now preached. We began spending more time together. Soon, romantic feelings began to stir. Friends cautioned me, but what I heard was judgment toward him rather than grace. All three of my children were against the relationship, including my two sons-in-law. I dug in my heels—my children couldn't tell me what to do! Sound familiar? I was certain that what he needed above all else was grace and a second chance. A new beginning. I was determined to be one who offered that to him.

I was not objective. I looked for what I wanted rather than seeking good advice. I even withdrew from those who tried to give me counsel to not entangle myself in the relationship. And I saw the Scriptures through my own subjective grid. I looked for signs that confirmed my decision and ignored the warning signs pointed out by those who cared so deeply about me. And then I made my choice. I chose the relationship I was counseled to avoid. I married my fourth husband.

It wasn't long before I realized things were not going well. The choice to marry him put a strain on my relationship with all three of my children. They could see what I couldn't. My new husband was only too happy to isolate me from my children.

Our relationship rapidly deteriorated.

One day, as he left the house to take his car to Richmond for service, he cursed at me with an extremely vulgar word. I had asked him to get a job. He had been unemployed for three years, and we were living on what I earned. He was capable of work. He had impressive educational degrees. He was physically able. But he made no effort to find work.

For him to curse me was very hurtful. Numb, I put on my "I'm fine" mask and went on about my work. It was the only way I knew how to survive. My wonderful assistant was due any minute, and I was not prepared to let her or anyone else know what was happening. I just needed to get my bearings. I sent up a quick arrow prayer: "Lord, help me." I didn't know how I was going to navigate another bad marriage. I felt numb. We'd been married not quite a year.

Tragic News

Later in the day, the phone rang. My assistant answered, and I heard her talking but wasn't listening. Then I heard her say, "Hold, please. I'll get her on the line." When I answered, a woman identified herself as a nurse at a hospital in Richmond. She told me there had been a bad accident and asked me several questions, then said I needed to bring my husband's medications to Richmond. On the way to the hospital, I asked God to help me do what He wanted me to do.

A police officer met me at the emergency room and took me up to the trauma floor. I had no idea what I was going to see, but I had a deep sense that I was in God's hands. A team of doctors met me at the elevator, had me sit down, and began a litany of my husband's injuries. It was overwhelming. I stopped them and asked if any of the injuries were life threatening. As I think back, I must have been in shock. Any one of his injuries was life threatening, much less the combination.

With my husband on life support, I knew this would be a long journey. Friends gathered. We met together in the conference room and prayed. Both of my girls came to be with me. They were supportive and loving.

I was with him in the ICU, day after day, for weeks after his catastrophic automobile accident, yet living with a heavy heart, knowing our relationship had been suffering severely even before the accident.

He lost his left arm. He was on a ventilator, respirator, and dialysis. While he was in the hospital, I found out I was in debt to the tune of one hundred thousand dollars—by his doing! It seemed unreal.

My husband was in the hospital for six weeks, then spent more weeks in rehab for a total of three months.

How could I move forward? I knew I had decisions to make. I began to make plans to sell the house to help pay off some of the debt. It all felt so overwhelming. Thankfully, I had the clear sense that I was in God's hands.

When my husband returned home, his verbal abusiveness increased. I tried to understand that his injuries were almost more than he could bear. But I also knew others who had suffered that and more but were not so angry, bitter, and abusive.

Sad Confirmation

Months passed. Privately, I expressed my concern to him that we were not communicating, and I was unhappy in our marriage. I felt as if he didn't love me and I was hurting. He was like Teflon, letting nothing I said stick. He didn't seem to hear what I said and didn't want to address the issues.

I decided to do my best to follow Jesus's instructions on the process of forgiveness in Matthew that says,

If another believer sins against you, go privately and point out the offense. If the other person listens and confesses it, you have won that person back. But if you are unsuccessful, take one or two others with you and go back again, so that everything you say may be confirmed by two or three witnesses. If the person still refuses to listen, take your case to the church. Then if he or she won't accept the church's decision, treat that person as a pagan or a corrupt tax collector. (18:15–17 NLT)

I'd gone to him privately. Now I confronted him before two elders in the church. They were two of his close friends who had stuck with him through all the legal trials and jail. We were in our living room. I'd written down the things, both positive and negative, that I wanted to say. It was as if he couldn't or wouldn't hear my heart's cry. Then he looked me straight in the eye and told me, "I never loved you." I was hurt, humiliated, and numb all at the same time. But at least he'd confirmed what I'd sensed for a long time.

I wept bitter tears. All my hopes and dreams for the marriage dissolved. My heart felt like lead. The familiar, sick pain of a doomed marriage roared back. My heart literally hurt with the grief and rejection. I had done all I knew to do to make the marriage work. I really wanted it to. I loved him. I gave pieces of myself away to try to make him happy. Thoughts like, *I've done it again*, and *How could I not have seen?* filled me with shame.

He announced that he wanted to divorce me. Under advice from my own pastor and two church elders, I met with a lawyer to draw up a separation agreement so he could do me no more financial damage. Several months later, he filed for divorce.

I knew I had to forgive him. But it was myself I had to forgive most of all. People had warned me, but I ignored their words, thinking they just didn't know him like I did. I'd told myself they didn't understand him, that my love for him would heal him, and that I could encourage him out of his troubled behavior. But I was the one who had refused to see the truth. I was the one who didn't comprehend the extensive damage of the choices he'd made before our marriage. I was the one who didn't listen to warnings. Yes, I was guilty. And filled with shame.

Forgive myself? Yes. I had to, to be able to move forward in a healthy way. But I didn't know what to do. I sought counseling. I prayed. I claimed promises. I tried to take care of myself—to exercise, continue to work, be with friends, go to good movies, read, play with my grandchildren. But there were moments it was overwhelming, and just moving forward consumed all my energy. I spent a lot of time in If-only-ville. If only I had heeded the warnings in my head. If only I had listened to others. If only I hadn't married him. If only . . .

The Core Issue

We've all probably heard the old adage that the definition of insanity is to repeatedly do the same thing but expect a different result. That is what I had done in marriage. I was crushed with shame. I had to seriously ask myself *why*, and my questions haunted me. Had I not learned the first time? Was something terribly wrong with me? What was it? Was I even saved?

Second Corinthians 5:17 says, "Therefore if anyone is in Christ, he is a new creature; the old things passed away: behold, new things have come." This verse is often quoted as if salvation ends our struggle—we are made new creations. But what about the past? Is there no damage and woundedness from the past that affect our present? Do we no longer experience doubt, fear, pain? After salvation, do we then do everything right? Have we been given a blank page to start over?

In many ways, our conversion is just the beginning of a lifelong process of growth. Yes, we are saved, but there is much work the Holy Spirit has to do in us. The theological word for this is *sanctification.* We are like onions with layer after layer of sin and brokenness to be brought to the surface and dealt with honestly before God. God deals with some people quickly. Others, like me, take time and lots of patience. Just when I think the blemished layers have all been removed, another layer is revealed. And to my great dismay, the same blemish is exposed yet again.

Perhaps you have felt the same way. Repeated a sin. You thought you'd never do it again, but you did and now you are back to square one. Feeling like a big failure. Full of guilt and shame. Like me, you can beat yourself up, get depressed, live in denial, get angry, and blame others. But that doesn't redeem your failures.

We know about redemption when it comes to Jesus dying on the cross for our sins, but what about redemption of our failures after we are Christians? Can they be redeemed?

Yielding to God's process in our lives involves a struggle with self. We are saved sinners, and as such we continue to sin even in our redemptive process. If you find yourself in such a place of repeating the same thing over and over, begin to ask yourself some tough questions and tell yourself the truth. Look for and discover your "core issue," as I call it. A core issue is the result of an experience or trauma in our life that shapes the way we think, feel, act, reason, and love. It may define how you think of yourself. It may define how you see yourself in many areas of your life. Perhaps the abuse you suffered. Some handicap. A betrayal that crushed you. A criticism that you let define you. The death of a parent or friend. An accident that altered your life. Someone you love who is an alcoholic or very controlling. Perhaps some fear you have nurtured. You may have overheard one of your parents or grandparents say they wished you had not been born, which resulted in your feeling that you don't really belong—you're always looking in from the outside. You feel inadequate in some way, and you feel very insecure or act out by being a bully. Or you feel you are better than others and are entitled.

We all have a core issue.

I wasn't aware of this, and I was blind to the issue that was driving me to the same poor choices again and again.

Until one day . . .

I was talking openly about my struggle as to why I kept making relationship mistakes with a good friend who knew me well and whom I trusted. He looked into my eyes and said, "You felt abandoned as a child." My eyes suddenly filled with tears, and I instantly knew he had hit a nerve. He had spoken truth. I did not want to admit it and tried to hide it, but he was right. I recognized the truth deep down in the dark recesses of my heart.

Yes, my core issue is abandonment.

Through the Eyes of a Child

I'm taking a deep breath even as I write these words because I long not to be misunderstood in what I am about to write. I do not seek to blame or rationalize my choices—please understand, I am very aware that *my choices were my own.* I, alone, am responsible for them. There are no excuses for acting out as we do, but sometimes there are reasons.

As a little girl, I read my father's absences as abandonment. I am in no way blaming him or saying he was a bad father. He didn't intentionally hurt me. Never. If he knew he had hurt me, it would have broken his heart. And I never told him. My father's love for me was gentle and kind and warm. It was just that my little girl heart read his frequent long absences as abandonment. And the feeling of abandonment developed in me a deep need for security. I sought to meet that need in unhealthy relationships rather than God. I had to tell myself the truth: my response to my absentee father was sinful.

My father put ministry before family. God gave him his family first, but he let the pressures of ministry take over—leaving his family sometimes for six months at a time. I felt as if when I needed him the most, he was the farthest away. He once estimated that, while we were growing up, he traveled over 50 percent of the time. And when he was home, he was tired and preoccupied and surrounded—by staff and those who needed him. There were others nearly constantly present with him and our family. A daughter of a former US president once told me, "Staff ruins intimacy." She was right. Privacy for long, thoughtful conversations or tender moments of intimate connection with my father was rare.

And a busy, distracted father can't spend much time develop-
ing a relationship with his quiet middle child.

Do I understand how it happened? Yes. Do I blame him?
No. He didn't hurt me intentionally. My father is my hero,
but he had feet of clay just like any other man. He said
himself that one of the mistakes he made through the years
was being away from his family too often. And his frequent
absences had serious repercussions in my life.

When I was a younger woman, if you had asked me, I
would have told you Jesus was my security. I believed it, but
it wasn't true deep down in the dark places of my heart.
I didn't trust Him to care for me. I didn't trust Him to be
there. Wasn't He busy and preoccupied with other people?
Weren't their needs more important to Him? Wasn't He just
too far away? Just like Daddy.

How did this core issue of abandonment shape my life?
I desperately looked for a place of security, where I belonged. Yes, I knew in my heart I belonged to God. I was
His child. I believed I was secure in His love. But was I? I
didn't feel it. I wanted affirmation from others and to be
significant to someone. But I kept making wrong choices.
I made the same mistakes over and over again, resulting in
hurt and more insecurity. It seemed to be a vicious cycle.
Wanting desperately to be liked, I became a people pleaser
on many levels. I looked for the wrong things in people.
I looked for them to meet my need. Based on my woundedness and need rather than God's love for me, I made
choices that all but guaranteed I would be wounded again.
And again.

How did I begin to break that cycle? The Bible says, "Faithful are the wounds of a friend" (Prov. 27:6). When my friend

identified my core issue that day, it was a turning point. I'd spent thousands of dollars on counseling over the years, and no one had ever identified it. Ever. But now it seemed so obvious. The piece fit! Now I was telling myself the truth.

Truth-telling means I need to realize, like an alcoholic, that I have to be vigilant and aware of what I am thinking and how I am responding to things. I have to be accountable to godly, praying people. We tend to think accountability is someone looking over our shoulder whom we have to explain ourselves to. People who will keep us on the defensive. We see it as a negative or rigorous discipline. But as I once heard Bob Goff say in conversation, "to be held accountable is to be held close." It means to listen to counsel and cling to God as never before. I have a small group of ladies who pray together regularly, and I ask them to hold me accountable. I am brutally honest with them and feel very safe. It is freeing, not scary, to have folks with whom I can bare my soul—the good, the bad, and the ugly.

My story is not finished. I am still on the journey. We are all works in process. There are areas in my life that are still broken. God in His grace doesn't reveal all the brokenness at one time; we would be devastated if that were the case! He reveals the places where we fall short slowly, over time—in His time and His way. There are still layers to be peeled away that need to be discarded. He is gentle with the wounded and broken. "A bruised reed will he not break, and a dimly burning wick will he not quench: he will bring forth justice in truth" (Isa. 42:3 ASV).

We are all broken. That is our condition.

I'd like to briefly look at the life of Samson. I think we can get some clues there for our own lives.

Samson

Samson was a hero. You might say he was the Incredible Hulk or Captain America of ancient Israel. Before he was conceived, he was destined for greatness. An angel of the Lord appeared to his barren mother and told her that she would bear a son, specially created and chosen by God, set apart for a specific purpose. "He shall begin to deliver Israel from the hands of the Philistines" (Judg. 13:5). God's messenger also said, "Now therefore, be careful not to drink wine or strong drink, nor eat any unclean thing. For behold, you shall conceive and give birth to a son, and no razor shall come upon his head, for the boy shall be a Nazirite to God from the womb" (vv. 4–5). The Torah stated that a Nazirite was marked by abstaining from alcohol, not cutting your hair, and prohibition from any contact with a dead body.

His mother named him Samson, which means, "sun" or "of the sun." What an apt name for someone who had such a bright future ahead of him! This little guy had a good, solid beginning, coming from God-fearing parents who worshiped and trusted the God of Israel. Sadly, a good beginning doesn't guarantee an equally good ending. Good beginnings can fool us into thinking we can be complacent when perseverance on a godly path is what is required. I'm not sure many people say, "I want to be like Samson." And I haven't heard many people name their son Samson—maybe their dog, but not a son! Perhaps this is because it certainly seems that he was not one of God's brightest stars, never reaching his full potential because he allowed sinful, selfish desires to rule over him. At times he used his God-given gift foolishly and in anger, and he gave up this gift in order to please a woman. He didn't learn his lesson from that disaster, and did it again.

Thankfully, God uses men and women who are horribly flawed and fail spectacularly, as evidenced by those mentioned in the "Hall of Faith" chapter in Hebrews. Samson is one of those named, having held the position of judge in Israel for twenty years. And yet, although Samson's role as judge involved convicting people of the sin of turning away from God and worshiping idols, delivering them from foreign powers, and administering justice to keep the people focused on God alone, he was unable to overcome the recurring sin stemming from his core issue in his own life. Just because he was a God-ordained judge and is listed in the Hall of Fame, he does not get a free pass for his sinful behavior. Scripture never skimps when it comes to revealing the real lives and real sin of our biblical heroes.

Probably Samson's strongest positive character quality was his passion—whatever stood before him, he was all in. But his strongest positive quality also brought him his worst downfall. He let his passion run amok rather than keeping it under the authority and control of the Lord. Instead of using God's standards as the criteria in making decisions and then allowing God to use his passion to complete his God-given and ordained tasks, he allowed the criteria for his decisions to come all too often from those unwieldy and wild passions.

When he saw a pretty woman, he wanted her and went after her. Plain and simple. When someone made him angry, he took revenge. As with all stories, Samson's is complicated, and we need to carefully read the Scripture to see where he was acting under the power of the Spirit of the Lord and when he was under the influence of his passion.

We all know the story of Samson and Delilah. Well, she was not the first woman he married. Against his parents' advice, he married a Philistine woman who caught his attention. That marriage ended badly for her. (See Judges 14 and 15 for the whole story.)

But Samson didn't learn to rein in his sexual appetite after that fiasco. He went to Gaza, and again saw a woman, a prostitute, and went to her. The people of Gaza planned to kill him, but he escaped. "At midnight he arose and took hold of the doors of the city gate and the two posts and pulled them up along with the bars; then he put them on his shoulders and carried them up to the top of the mountain which is opposite Hebron" (Judg. 16:3).

He became a legend throughout the land. Everyone heard of his superhuman strength. *But what is the secret behind it*, they wondered.

Sometime later he fell in love again, this time with a woman named Delilah. The leaders of the Philistines went to Delilah and offered her an astronomical sum of money to betray Samson. She was in relationship with a legend, but she didn't value or respect him—she valued money more.

Three times Delilah whined, cried, and begged Samson to give her the secret of his great strength, and three times he gave her false information. You'd think alarm bells would have gone off in his brain and he'd realize what she was doing when each false method was tried out by the Philistines. But he didn't catch on. After the third attempt, she appealed to his weakest point—his passion. She hit him with, "How can you say, 'I love you,' when your heart is not with me? You have deceived me these three times and have not told me where your great strength is" (v. 15).

He still refused to reveal the true reason for his strength until "she pressed him daily with her words and urged him, that his soul was annoyed to death" (v. 16). And so he told her.

He fell asleep on her lap, and the Philistines came in and shaved off his hair. When he awoke, "he did not know that the LORD had departed from him" (v. 20). They gouged out his eyes. They bound him in bronze shackles. They put him in prison and set him to grinding grain.

Over time, no one paid any attention to his hair. It was growing back, and with it, his strength.

One evening his enemies threw a party in honor of offering a sacrifice to their god, Dagon, and decided Samson would be their entertainment. As he was forced to perform for them, three thousand people looked down from the rooftop and mocked and jeered at the "great Samson."

Samson asked the servant assigned to lead him to place him where he could lean against the support pillars of the house. He then called out to God what would have been a fabulous prayer—except what he wanted was for his wounded body and pride to be vindicated. "Self" had never been dealt with in Samson's core—it was still there. "Then Samson called to the LORD and said, 'O Lord GOD, please remember me and please strengthen me just this time, O God, that I may at once be avenged of the Philistines for my two eyes'" (v. 28). Avenging himself for his eyes. Not God's glory. Not God's power. But Samson's *eyes*.

But God answered his prayer anyway. Nothing can rob God of His glory. Samson placed his right hand on one pillar, his left hand on another, and pushed with all his might. The temple collapsed, killing all three thousand people—those inside as well as those on the roof. Samson died with his enemies.

A sad ending to a great beginning.

Your Weakness Turned to Strength

Samson's core issue was his unbridled passion. He was all about passion in the moment. He was so controlled by his passion that he lost his sense of purpose. Therefore, he didn't keep commitments. He did what was convenient for him and indulged himself. He cared only to please himself.

Samson kept the wrong company and gave away his honor and integrity to manipulative women. He was driven by his selfish physical desires and played fast and loose with his sacred vow. He didn't learn from his mistakes but repeated them until they destroyed him. He didn't set firm boundaries. He extracted revenge in his own time and his own way, rationalizing and making excuses for his actions.

Samson mishandled the great promises God had given his parents. His choices had dire consequences that affected those around him. The sad truth is that Samson repeatedly stepped over the line into immoral behavior, and it cost him his sight, his influence, and finally his life. Samson lost his battle with selfish passion—if he even tried to battle it. He is an example of how giving up the battles against our sin is a dangerous place to be spiritually.

I struggle to understand why God used Samson to judge Israel for twenty years when he couldn't manage his own life. Why would God use such a flawed individual?

Hebrews 11:32–34 gives us a clue where it says,

> And what more shall I say? For time will fail me if I tell of Gideon, Barak, Samson, Jephthah, of David and Samuel and the prophets, who by faith conquered kingdoms, performed acts of righteousness, obtained promises, shut the mouths of lions, quenched the power of fire, escaped the edge of the sword, *from weakness were made strong,* became mighty in war, put foreign armies to flight. (emphasis added)

And the story of Samson also shows that just because we don't have it together in one area of our lives doesn't mean God can't use us in another. God kept His promises to Samson's parents and fulfilled His purposes. God can use even our weaknesses to glorify Himself. For that I am grateful!

I can see myself in Samson. I too have made repeated mistakes. I wanted what I wanted. I gave my integrity to another. I let another manipulate me. I didn't want to wait for God's best for me. I didn't want others to tell me the truth. I didn't tell myself the truth. I couldn't handle the truth. All to my detriment. That is a dangerous place to be spiritually.

Like Samson, I have sinned. I wondered what was wrong with me. I have lived with shame and regret. I have shed buckets of tears. I had more questions than answers. Had I out-sinned God's grace? Had God abandoned me?

No. His grace is real. I fell on God's loving grace, knowing God was going to work out His purpose in my life for His glory. That's what mattered most to me.

Are you able to identify your core issue? Look for it. Find it. Confess it. You may need a wise friend, counselor, or pastor—someone who has known you a long time and who loves you—to help you identify your core issue. Are you able to tell yourself the truth—the hard truth—about what drives you to repeat the same mistake over and over again? Commit to honesty with yourself and others. Forgiveness is realistic and honest. Forgiveness and truth-telling go hand in hand. Forgiveness requires that we ask ourselves *How did I contribute to this? Did I enable this situation?* Forgiveness confronts the wrongs done to us and by us.

I knew that telling myself the truth would mean a rock-bottom assessment of myself and looking at things I didn't want to see. But if I wanted to forgive myself, I needed to start there. I wanted God to use my lack of judgment, my sin, to teach me about myself. I took comfort that God uses even our weaknesses to glorify Himself. God is always teaching. I was ready to learn. He is always moving toward His purpose in our lives. I was ready to move forward.

ELEVEN

Going Backward to Go Forward

It is only as we allow the wounds of our past to be reopened that the pain can be identified and healed.

John Bishop

My friend John Bishop once told me a story about a man visiting the circus. He saw a big elephant tethered by a very small chain. He approached the trainer and asked him, "How does that small chain hold such a large creature?" The trainer replied, "It doesn't. But the elephant doesn't know that."

Then the trainer explained that when the elephant was small, a chain was put on his ankle. It was strong enough to hold him then because he was a baby elephant. As he grew, they continued to use the same chain. When he became an adult, he was much stronger than the chain and could easily break it—but didn't try. The trainer added, "It's not the chain that holds him but the memory of the chain."

Thanks to my friend's insight about my struggle with abandonment, I realized that I too had a chain around my ankle that was holding me back. A double chain, really. The first was self-condemnation over repeating the same old broken pattern of seeking unhealthy marital relationships. The second was guilt over the fact that I had abandonment issues. After all, I had wonderful parents—truly gifted and amazing people. Pillars of faith who, while being loving parents, loved and served God with all their hearts. They passed a rich legacy of faith and love on to me. With such a solid foundation, how could I possibly struggle with issues of abandonment? And yet, I did.

So I went to see a counselor. We talked about many things. He asked good questions, hard questions. He confronted my carefully constructed defensive shield. It was uncomfortable, and I didn't like it. I soon discovered that I compartmentalized my life and emotions so I wouldn't be vulnerable to others.

One day my counselor suggested that, in prayer, I go back and picture Jesus in the living room with me when my husband said that he never loved me. What might Jesus say to me as I heard those words?

Go back?

That's the last thing I wanted to do!

And that's when I knew how Hagar must have felt.

Hagar's Choice

God specifically promised Abram a son—an heir—of his own flesh and blood. Abram believed God, though, humanly

184

speaking, pregnancy was impossible; he and Sarai had no children and were well past the child-bearing years. But Abram believed, and God counted it as righteousness.

I can only imagine what it was like when Abram reported to Sarai what the Lord had told him. At long last they would have their child! As they waited in expectant hope, they got everything ready for this promised child. In their excitement, did they tell everyone about God's promise? When time passed and nothing seemed to be happening, they must have tired of the questions. "When shall we see joy for you?" "Do you have happy news yet?"

They waited and waited and waited. But no baby came.

Over time, the questions changed to glances of pity. Whispers behind shielded hands. Surely God had cursed them with this barrenness.

Sarai and Abram asked questions of their own. "Have we heard God correctly?" "Is a baby going to come?" "Have we made a mistake?"

Frustration and sadness began to fill the air between them. A growing whine in Sarai's voice and, eventually, anger as she blamed God for keeping her from having children (Gen. 16:2). It's possible her prayers took on a demanding tone. "God, why haven't You given us a child? Fulfill Your promise to us!"

When God didn't come through in her timing and her way, Sarai looked to her own understanding and concluded that perhaps God needed her help, and she took matters into her own hands.

She went to her husband and told him her plan—that he should sleep with her servant, Hagar, in order to build a family through her. In those ancient times, maidservants were considered property and legal extensions of their mistress, and thus could legally bear children in the name of the mistress. Perhaps Abram agreed simply because it wasn't that unusual of a practice. Or perhaps Sarai planted the idea that if God promised him a child of his own flesh and blood, then surrogacy was the way God intended to accomplish that feat. Or perhaps he was just tired of her complaining. Whatever the reason was, the Bible doesn't say. We only know that Abram went along with her plan.

Thus, Sarai gave Hagar to Abram "as a wife." Hagar had no say in this at all. She was just a possession, used as her owners saw fit.

Abram slept with her and she conceived.

Ah, now the slave had something over her mistress. Hagar had managed what Sarai could not—she was pregnant with the master's heir! She reveled in the fact that she, not Sarai, was carrying Abram's child. She was cruel to her mistress. The Bible says, "her mistress was despised in her sight" (v. 4). Merriam-Webster's dictionary defines *despise* as to regard as negligible, worthless, or distasteful.[1]

This was too much for Sarai. She became angry with Abram, stomping into his presence to shout, "You are responsible for the wrong I am suffering." (Go figure! He had only gone along with *her* plan.) "May the LORD judge between you and me," she said (v. 5), basically declaring, "God will tell us who is right (and I bet it will be me)."

Abram didn't show much leadership in this mess. He shrugged and said something like, "Not my problem. She's your servant. You do as you see fit," offering no protection for Hagar, the mother of his child. But Hagar wasn't without blame, either.

Here we have a furious wife; a gloating, pregnant, hormonal servant; and a clueless husband who doesn't want to involve himself in the ways of women. What a messy, miserable household! I can only imagine the snipping and sarcasm, the blame and whining, the bickering, the anger and tears. Two unhappy women and one man who cannot figure it out and so passes off his responsibility of leadership.

Then Sarai saw fit to deal with Hagar with what seems overabundant harshness. Sarai treated her so badly that Hagar fled into the desert, choosing the dangers of little water, no protection, and no shelter rather than suffering under the bitterness of her mistress. She was hurt and confused. The wilderness was not a good choice—but to her it seemed better than Sarai's tent.

While she was in the wilderness, next to a spring of water, the angel of the Lord came to her and asked where she had come from and where she was going. Of course, he already knew she was running away from the misery in Sarai and Abram's household. I think he wanted Hagar to be honest and acknowledge where she was and what had happened. He wanted her to examine herself.

She answered him honestly, telling him she was "fleeing from the presence of my mistress Sarai" (v. 8) because she could no longer live in Sarai's tent with the harshness and bitterness. She used the word *fleeing*, which has a sense of urgency and fear—she was desperate to get away.

But she didn't answer his second question because she didn't know where she was going. She hadn't thought that far ahead. She was just reacting to the misery in the household. She had done what seemed best to her—just like Sarai had done. In response, the angel didn't put his arm around her and say, "There, there. I don't blame you. Sarai is a bitter old woman. Let me help you get settled in this barren place." No. What did he tell her?

"Return to your mistress and submit yourself to her authority" (v. 9).

Go back? And submit to Sarai? That was the last thing Hagar expected to hear or wanted to do. But God made her a promise—that if she obeyed, she would have many descendants. She would go from being a helpless slave on the run in the wilderness to being the mother of nations.

Now it was up to Hagar. Could Hagar trust Sarai and Abram's God to take care of her when all seemed lost? Would she believe in the promise God gave? Would she go back?

God told Hagar to go back to the place that was hard. To leave what looked like freedom—her own understanding, her new comfort zone—and go back to where things began to go wrong. In essence, I believe He was saying, "Hagar, you cannot expect to build a secure future when there is unfinished business in your life. Trust Me for this 'going back.'"

And she did. She now had faith in a God who sees and cares—even about an Egyptian servant girl. And she obeyed that same God who saw and cared about her.

None of us like that word, *obedience*, and I'm guessing Hagar didn't like it much either. But it is the key to our spiritual growth. She could have remained in the wilderness with excuses and blame. But she chose to obey, recognizing God's presence for herself. The Bible says, "Thereafter, Hagar used another name to refer to the LORD, who had spoken to her. She said, 'You are the God who sees me'" (v. 13 NLT). She no longer had a relationship with Him through Sarai or anyone else. She now knew God for *herself*. She now had her own personal relationship with God. She wasn't a pawn in the dynamics between Sarai and Abram. She had her own purpose. God had a plan for *her* life. And it was good.

Hagar obeys and things are different, maybe not in Sarai's tent but inside Hagar. God had something bigger in mind for Hagar; He wanted to build a nation. And God fulfilled His promise to her to have more descendants than she could count. (The Arab nations are Hagar's descendants.)

What if she had not obeyed?

God told Jacob to go back and face Esau, whom he feared. On the way, he became a changed man. What if he had not obeyed? Paul went back to Lystra, where he had been stoned. And the church grew. What if he had not obeyed? Onesimus went back to Philemon and found a brother. What if he had not obeyed? The prodigal went back to face his father. He found a new relationship as a forgiven, welcomed son, and so we have a powerful picture of how God forgives us: unconditionally, graciously. What if he had not returned?

Where do *you* go to flee a bad situation? Where is your wilderness? Is it the land of old memories of pain and hurt? Wherever you flee, God sees you. He sees you in that pain. He sees you in your past. In your now. And yes, in your future. You can be sure that God will find you and see you, even in your wilderness. Psalm 139:7–12 says,

> Where can I go from Your Spirit?
> Or where can I flee from Your presence?
> If I ascend to heaven, You are there;
> If I make my bed in Sheol, behold, You are there.
> If I take the wings of the dawn,
> If I dwell in the remotest part of the sea,

Even there Your hand will lead me,
And Your right hand will lay hold of me.
If I say, "Surely the darkness will overwhelm me,
And the light around me will be night,"
Even the darkness is not dark to You,
And the night is as bright as the day.
Darkness and light are alike to You.

And when God reveals Himself to you in your wilderness, He will ask your obedience. How will you respond?

Sometimes we have to go backward to go forward and discover what God wants us to see there. When God leads us to do so, He has something much bigger in mind. He meets us there. He has a purpose, and it is good.

Moving Forward While Looking Backward

The thought of going back in my mind to revisit that hurtful encounter with my now ex-husband seemed ugly on so many levels. I knew Jesus was with me because He lives in me, but I'd never thought of Him as actually *there*, seeing what was happening to me. What would He say? Would He blame me too? I did not want to go back. I struggled at the thought of it. But I wanted freedom more. Each day, I tried to settle myself, clear my mind of distractions, breathe deeply, and ask the Holy Spirit to guide me.

Over time, little by little, I could see Jesus in that living room with me. Hurting for me. Loving me. The "God who sees me" was tender and kind. He didn't condemn me. He empathized with me. He assured me that He'd nailed my hurt and shame to the cross. He hated what happened but

Going Backward to Go Forward

let me know He cherished me, delighted in me, and washed me clean. I pictured Him holding me afterward, letting me cry while telling Him how I felt. His presence was real. His comfort was transformative.

Yes, I still have to remind myself to renew my mind with His Word as I recall the incident, but the pain and shame are gone. Jesus set me free from all of it. Satan can no longer use it against me.

Now that I had "gone back" and relived the encounter with my husband, it was time for the next step. It was time to "go back" to the origins of my sense of abandonment.

You need to understand here the depth of my love for my father. I adored him then and still adore the memory of him. I didn't want to think I had been abandoned. I didn't want to admit that I needed to forgive my father.

The thought of going back to the days of his absences in my youth and examining their impact on me was an overwhelming thought. There was a reason I'd buried those feelings. Was I ready to face them? It seemed it would have been much easier to keep the mask on and keep pretending it didn't matter—that I took it all in stride. But I didn't like what I felt—a sense of being "less than." Less than whole. Less than worthy. Less than known. I didn't want to continue to be broken. Dr. David Stoop said, "The high value that is placed on family and respect for parents makes it almost impossible for children to integrate their parents' failings and weaknesses."[2] That was where I was.

Yet I knew my answer to God's call to go back had to be yes. I believed in God's promises for me, that He had plans for me, plans to prosper me and not to harm me; plans to give me a future and a hope (see Jer. 29:11). If I was going to move forward in my spiritual life rather than continue to repeat the broken patterns based on my fear of abandonment, I needed to see my father's actions not through the eyes of the child I had been but through the eyes God had given me now—the eyes of an adult who lives in grace. But I had to start with what I experienced as a child.

A Daughter's Memories

At first, it was scary. Satan hissed his lies and accusations to keep me bound to fear, pretense, and self-effort. But I really wanted to be free, so I pressed on.

I remember as a young child asking Mother if they had adopted me. She said, "No, of course not." But I felt different from my siblings. The proof of it, I feared, was that my baby book was empty. Of course, with the third child, the baby book is always empty. But I didn't know that at the time. And of course, when Franklin was born as the fourth child, he was the first boy and "Billy Junior." At that point I felt I had become invisible—a feeling that stuck with me through the rest of my childhood and adolescence.

I don't recall having much individual time with just my father when I was a child. Whenever we went out to dinner or were out in public, Daddy was always busy with other people. He rarely focused on me. I didn't see it as his fault—people always crowded in—and it didn't make me angry; it's just the way it was.

In my memories, Daddy was absent far more than he was present. Once in a while I know we'd get on the phone with him, but I don't remember many times. Long-distance phone calls were difficult and expensive in those days. But I do know that whenever he could phone, he called Mother every day and his own mother as often as he was able. He was very good about that. But I wondered, Did he think of me while he was gone? I didn't know.

Certainly, God blessed the ministry my father was doing around the globe. But the cost at home was high. Yes, God supplied us with wonderful friends, team members, and mentors along the way who were like family. There were others who also helped fill the gap left by my father's absences. But no one can substitute for your own father. I knew I was loved. But as a little girl, I craved to have him home to tuck me into bed at night and pick me up whenever I skinned my knee. He wasn't there. I felt his absence keenly.

Looking back, I could see that I was constantly looking for security. Even in grade school, I always wanted a boyfriend—wanted to be special to somebody. Each year I would have someone I cared about. I usually chose people stronger than me, both in friendships and romantic relationships. People who were in control. I felt safe with them.

When I reached ninth grade I was sent to a boarding school in Florida. Soon I felt like I belonged there. I had bouts of homesickness but adjusted well, and it wasn't long before I had a boyfriend. I do recall that while there, a member of my father's team, T. W. Wilson—"Uncle T"—also had a daughter attending the same school. Several times, Daddy and Uncle T came to visit together and we would go off for a weekend. I reveled in that!

After two years, my parents took me out of the school I was happy in and transferred me to Stony Brook Girls' School on Long Island to be near my brother, who was enrolled in The

Stony Brook School. I had a severe case of mononucleosis at the time, but Mother took me there, got me settled in the infirmary at school, and left me. Then she flew to Europe to join my father. I was quite ill and recall feeling very lonely. I was a Southern girl surrounded by sophisticated New York girls—a fish out of water.

I have no memory of either of my parents ever visiting me at that school.

From Stony Brook I went to Gordon College at the early age of sixteen. Since I had been so miserable at Stony Brook and didn't want to go into public school at that late point in my school career, my father arranged for me to attend Gordon, where I could finish my senior year of high school by correspondence while doing my freshman year at Gordon. Mother and I flew to New York, where she wanted to buy me a warm winter coat, knowing the New England weather was harsher than I was accustomed to. She then dropped me off at college. I didn't know anybody. Again, I felt very insecure and out of place. I didn't even know what I wanted to study. Because Mother always said being a wife and a mother was the highest calling you can have, I think it was my subconscious goal to find a husband.

My roommate turned out to be a godsend. She and I are still friends and talk regularly. We came from totally different worlds, but she accepted me and included me in her circle. It was a wonderful feeling. She and her family embraced me. They had a modest home in Maine near the water, and I was invited there a number of times. We'd go to the dock and get lobsters for lunch—I'd never had "lobstah." They incorporated me into their family. Her parents were like parents to me. I could be myself with them. Though they called and wrote letters, I don't recall that Mother or Daddy ever visited me while I was at Gordon.

While attending Gordon, I got reacquainted with a man I'd met before—the man who would become my first husband. He wasn't a student there, but his sister was. (He was in business with his father.) He would come and visit her, and our relationship blossomed. I felt secure with him. He had a very strong personality and the means to take care of me. We married when I was eighteen. It seemed I'd always been looking for a home—a place to feel secure and securely loved. Instead I'd chosen men who couldn't provide that security for me. So I was repeatedly abandoned.

I am not blaming my parents for my choices in men. I made those choices myself. Looking back, I could see that it was sin born out of my neediness that led to my own unhealthy ways to meet my need for security. I came to understand where the root for my insecurity was, and it freed me to address the issue in my own heart and life so I didn't have to keep making the same mistakes.

A Father's Regrets

In the midst of my healing process, the Lord provided me with a gripping podcast by theologian Dr. R. T. Kendall on the topic of forgiving oneself. I've included the citation in the endnotes, and I highly recommend that you listen to it for yourself.[3] I was mesmerized as he spoke, and God used it to truly set me free over my issues with my father.

Dr. Kendall tells of when he first went to Oxford for what he planned to be a three-year stay to earn his doctorate degree. His supervisor gave him some surprising advice. "Don't forget your children. These years will go by quickly and you won't get them back." But Dr. Kendall, by his own admission, didn't heed that advice. At the end of the three years he was invited to become the minister at Westminster Chapel, London, and again he was too involved with the ministry to have time with his children.

Twenty-five years later, he retired filled with "a depth of guilt over my neglect of my children." He was invited by my father to be interviewed in a sixty-minute video, in which he said,

> For the last twenty-five years I put the church first thinking I was putting God first. I put sermon preparation first thinking I was putting God first. I now believe that had I put my family first I would have preached just as well. But I can't get those years back.[4]

In his book *How to Forgive Ourselves Totally*, Dr. Kendall wrote,

> My own problems with totally forgiving myself are rooted largely in my feelings of failure as a parent. . . . If I could turn back the clock I would have spent more time with my children. You have no idea the sense of guilt I have struggled with over this. And yes it is also what has helped me most to be sympathetic with people who have a problem forgiving themselves.[5]

I have to wonder if my father felt a similar guilt. I don't remember Daddy ever saying to me, "I'm so sorry I was gone so often." But he wrote more than once that one of his biggest regrets was that he didn't spend more time with his family. In his memoir, *Just As I Am*, he wrote,

> The BGEA and the Team became my second family without my realizing it. Ruth says those of us who were off traveling missed the best part of our lives—enjoying the children as they grew. She is probably right. I was too busy preaching all over the world. . . . For myself, as I look back, I now know I came through those years much the poorer both psychologically and emotionally. I missed so much by not being home to see the children grow and develop. The children must carry scars of those separations too.[6]

Daddy was right. I do carry those scars. But my heart is tender for my father. How sad that in all he gave to so many he should have suffered any regrets at all.

A New Point of View

Once I'd revisited my sad memories of feeling abandoned and given them to the Lord in healing prayer, I was able to begin to restore those memories and see them in a new light. God called my parents for a unique ministry at a unique time in the church's history. Post–World War II, in the middle of the twentieth century, after D. L. Moody, R. A. Torrey, and Aimee Semple McPherson, there were those seeking to address social issues confronting the church but neglecting evangelism. My father stepped into that void.

The opportunity and need were great. God guided both him and my mother into that ministry—him away so often and her at home with the children. We grew up seeing that as part of who we were. My mother wholeheartedly supported my father's ministry. She never complained about his being gone or made us feel short-changed. She always talked of the privilege we had of being his children and having a front-row seat to what God was doing.

There were many ways in which Mother worked to instill in us a sense of shared ministry. Whenever Daddy left our home in Montreat, we'd all go to the Black Mountain train station to see him off. We'd make a party of it! All sorts of people would show up at the train station to see him off. My grandparents, Daddy's secretary, community folks, friends, and some staff who worked for us. We'd all wave goodbye as the train rolled out of the station. Even the train porters knew who we were. They seemed to enjoy having "the Reverend" on their train.

When Daddy came home, we would reverse it all—we'd all gather at the station and wait with eager anticipation. We children would try to see who could catch a glimpse of the headlight of the train first when it came around the bend. Then we'd jump up and down and cheer. Sometimes we were so eager to see him, we'd go down the mountain to the Old Fort station so as to greet him one stop earlier.

I don't remember ever being sad when Daddy left. I think I took my cues from Mother. She set the tone, and we all followed suit. She never said, "Poor me." She must have been lonely. She once wrote that she used to sleep with one of Daddy's shirts so she could have his smell. I'm sure it was very hard for both of them. But they never revealed it. Of course, they would have very much believed that hiding their sadness was the right thing to do. Back in the fifties, people didn't talk about their feelings very much.

Certainly, I wouldn't say that Daddy traveling the world with the gospel was wrong, but now I had to ask the hard question: What was their real first ministry? God gave them family. Isn't it God first, family second, and ministry third? Well, in the late 1940s and 1950s it wasn't thought of that way; God came first and ministry came second. Home was third. One need only look at the patterns of countless missionaries during that period who placed their children in boarding schools so they could follow their mission. This is simply what was done by many.

Over the years, I've had many conversations with adult children of pastors and missionaries and I've seen that my experience was not unique. Countless children of those in ministry had to deal with feelings of coming in second or third place to ministry. When I meet young pastors and Christian leaders today who understand the importance of placing a high priority on nurturing their children during their ministry years, I applaud them for it.

A Healing Process

As I healed from my memories, I was able to begin to put them in perspective. The simple truth is that we live in a fallen, broken world. No parents are perfect, mine included. When Adam and Eve disobeyed God and yielded to the temptation to be more than God created them to be, they became broken, losing their wholeness, unity, and completeness. Fear and shame entered.

They lost their capacity to rightly enjoy God's good gifts. Perfection was replaced with pain. A joyful marriage became an unequal partnership. Happy cultivation became sweaty toil. The beautiful garden became a briar patch. Once-imperishable bodies began slowly to decay and die. And they were thrust out of their garden home forever. Everything that was once so good was turned on its head.[7]

Daddy, with Mother's full support, was leading a global ministry under the power of the Holy Spirit. Through that ministry God called countless souls into heaven. What a priceless contribution to the kingdom! They gave of themselves sacrificially. In the midst of that they reared five children. They loved each of us dearly and were faithful and true to one another without fail. Truly, I have so much for which to be grateful. My heart is full of love for them. I am one of only five in the world who were honored to be their children. Just as Mother said, we did have a front-row seat to some of God's amazing history! Sure, I feel sadness for what we all missed out on, but I believe God will make it up to us one day. Or perhaps it simply will no longer matter.

My going back to deal with my memories and sense of abandonment wasn't a quick process confined to a few counseling sessions. It took years. In the process of healing, God grew bigger in my eyes. He gave me the grace to identify the abandonment, the insight to identify how the enemy was trying to use it, and the courage to deal with it. It then became much easier to repent and experience God's gracious forgiveness and healing. Like I said earlier, we have to speak the truth before forgiveness can be fully experienced. I had to tell myself the truth. Once I did, it was so much better. Sins and hurts grow bigger in the dark. Once light reveals the truth, healing takes place. Like the light of sunshine can bring healing and growth, so does the truth of God's light.

Over time, I could finally accept that I had felt abandoned and it was time to forgive my father for that abandonment. I understood why it happened. I understood how it happened. I understood the necessity for his travel. Now I also understood and accepted how it affected me. I think it is in the acceptance that we can move on. To move to a place of acceptance is essential in healing and forgiveness. I no longer nurse my old wounds. They have been healed. (Otherwise I couldn't write so openly about them.)

Deep down in all of us is the hunger to be fully known. Understood. Accepted. Valued and loved. To belong. Now I could see that though I didn't find that deep sense of belonging at home as a child, today it was up to me to seek to have those needs met as a mature Christian believer. Rather than latching on to a controlling friend or a husband to meet that need, I needed to go to God—Father, Son, and Holy Spirit—to have those needs met. God and God alone is flawless. He loves me with an everlasting love, and He alone can meet my needs perfectly. He has given us His body—the community of believers with all the gifts of the Holy Spirit distributed—through whose fellowship we can enjoy some measure of that sense of belonging.

Of course, I need to keep in mind that the body is made of imperfect people like me, so I can't expect perfection there! But the fact that we are all forgiven unites us. My responsibility is to plug myself into His body, contribute my own gifts, and enjoy being ministered to by the gifts of others. I am a member of the family of God—to give and to receive by the grace of God. Today, the small group of women whom

I pray with and share accountability with is an example of the body meeting those needs.

Breaking Free of Our Chains

We all have painful memories from our past. Ones we'd like to forget, bury, and deny. Maybe they are lurking just under the surface like a black mold, ready to undermine all we so carefully tried to build as we sought to immerse ourselves in work and pleasure and relationships. We don't want to think about them. They bring shame. Heartache. They undermine the "self" we have built and threaten our carefully constructed personas.

We are all fundamentally broken and are in search of wholeness. We feel incomplete, longing for more but yet unsure of what that might be. We search in all sorts of ways to feel complete—relationships, money, education, position, status, fame—but find none truly fill the gap. We still feel incomplete. We long to be whole. In order to move toward wholeness, we need to examine ourselves; even the deep, hidden, broken places. As it says in Psalm 51:6, "Behold, You desire truth in the innermost being, and in the hidden part You will make me know wisdom."

We need the good news of the gospel to shine His light of truth brightly into our "hidden part." It alone can bring freedom, peace, joy, and renewal. Through the healing touch of our loving Savior we can be set free, experience peace, find purpose, and finally know completeness.

Taking the gospel to the deep, hidden, secret places in our hearts is a journey that can be painful, but the rewards are worth it. We'd like nothing better than to say, "Let bygones be bygones," put on a happy face, live in denial, get busy, and find the appropriate Scriptures to quote. We protect our vulnerable places with all sorts of methods. We compartmentalize, shutting the door so those memories don't bleed into other areas of our life. But they do, because the past is part of today. Like the chain on the elephant's ankle, we remember and are held back from stepping outside the familiar.

To help you in your own healing journey, I highly recommend Dr. Terry Wardle, who writes powerfully and practically about this transformative prayer process in his book *Wounded: How to Find Wholeness and Inner Healing in Christ.* Two other books that were influential in my healing were *Healing for Damaged Emotions* by David A. Seamonds and *Transformation of the Inner Man* by John L. Sandford. I was blessed to not only have a godly counselor but a trusted prayer partner as well. She and I prayed through John Sandford's book together.

I invite you to go back to your painful places, for when you do you will learn more about God. You will find a bigger God. Examine your past to build a better future.

How do you get started? For me, the journey began with recognizing my crippling regret. After years of denial and excuses, pretending to be what I wasn't, trying to meet the expectations of others, doing it my way, reaping the whirlwind of poor choices and repeated sins, I'd had enough. So I got the help I needed.

Do you feel a tug on your heart to make the same decision? Is there a place you need to return to? Maybe not a literal place but a situation that needs your attention? A fractured relationship that needs to be addressed, a sin that needs to be acknowledged, a lie that needs to be corrected, a hurt in your past that needs to be healed? Maybe you don't know what the issue is, but you know something isn't right.

What is God saying to you?

What chain has you bound to your past? Will you address it? Or do you want to be like the elephant—chained to your memory?

As we examine our lives before a holy and loving God who is tender with us, we find we are loved more than we ever dreamed. We find freedom to live authentically, freedom to be our true selves. I found that I could move from the shadows of the past into the light of God's grace and purpose. May you do the same.

TWELVE

What If I Still Can't Forgive?

If God forgives us we must forgive ourselves otherwise it's like setting up ourselves as a higher tribunal
than him.

C. S. Lewis

I once had a lovely pink cashmere sweater my husband had
given me for Christmas. I paired it with a flowing navy-
blue skirt with pink flowers. The sweater was a favorite of
mine. It was soft, comfortable, and just the right shade of
pastel pink to complement my skin tones. One spring day
while wearing it, I was in a jewelry store and leaned over the
counter to look at some of the jewelry. I stood next to a beautiful floral arrangement of lilies, enjoying their fragrance
that filled the store. Then I noticed that some bright yellow
lily pollen had attached itself to the sleeve of my sweater. I
brushed at it with my hand and, to my surprise, it smeared
into a yellow blotch.

When I got home, I changed clothes and lightly wiped at the stain with a damp cloth. The yellow blotch didn't budge. If anything, once it was wet it looked even worse. I applied some pre-treatment stain remover and let it sit before I hand-washed it. When I pulled it out of the basin, the pollen stain stared back at me defiantly. Determined not to be beaten, I applied a bit of laundry detergent directly to it and gently massaged the detergent into the stain, let it sit for a bit, then went back to it and rinsed it under running water, rubbing the detergent-soaked stain. But it was still there. *I'll let it soak longer*, I thought, applying more stain remover and immersing the sleeve in a basin of water. As the afternoon wore on, I repeatedly treated, soaked, and rubbed, all to no avail.

Finally, I realized that removing this stain was beyond my skills, so I set the sweater aside to take to the dry cleaners. I'd leave it for the professionals. Fortunately, they were able to remove the stain, and I wore the sweater for several more years before age got the best of it.

In his book *Set Free by Forgiveness*, J. Randall O'Brien writes, "What do we do when the wash is done but a stubborn stain remains?" I believe most of us do just what I did. We work hard to remove that stain. He continues, "What might we do with a sin that seems impossible to wash from our memory? What do we do when general forgiveness clothes us, but the lack of self-forgiveness in one tortuous area makes us feel naked and ashamed?"[1] His analogy is a good one.

So, what are you going to do if you've come this far in this book and find that you still can't forgive some person, or perhaps even yourself? What is your plan if the title of this chapter is exactly where you are right now? Will you throw in the towel and simply declare that this book "didn't work" for you? I hope not! In fact, as I write I am praying that no reader simply quits, choosing to continue to carry the pain and weight of unforgiveness. You are not beyond hope. You are, instead, right where God knew you would be at this point. He sees you. He knows what is in your heart. And He knows exactly where He wants to take you.

Let's begin with some good news: God is not mad at you!

God Is Not Mad at You

"Therefore there is now no condemnation for those who are in Christ Jesus," says Romans 8:1. You can believe that. God is not planning a way to punish you for your unforgiveness. All punishment was heaped on Jesus on the cross. You are already forgiven, even for your unforgiveness!

"But you were washed, but you were sanctified, but you were justified in the name of the Lord Jesus Christ and in the Spirit of our God," says 1 Corinthians 6:11. God didn't give up and leave your soul stained with sin. He got every stain out with the ultimate stain remover—the blood of Jesus.

Titus 3:4–5 tells us, "But when the kindness of God our Savior and His love for mankind appeared, He saved us, not on the basis of deeds which we have done in righteousness, but according to His mercy, by the washing of regeneration and renewing by the Holy Spirit." You don't have to earn God's approval by forgiving the one who wronged you. Your salvation is dependent only on the sacrifice of Jesus Christ.

Remember that God is an expert at forgiveness. Though you may be stuck right now in your struggle with forgiveness, you need to remember that God is at work. He is completing

His work in you. He just isn't finished with you yet! How do I know this? Because of this wonderful promise:

> In all my prayers for all of you, I always pray with joy because of your partnership in the gospel from the first day until now, being confident of this, that he who began a good work in you will carry it on to completion until the day of Christ Jesus. (Phil. 1:4–6 NIV)

It is God who has begun the work of forgiveness in your life, and He is the One who is going to complete that work in you. He wants the very best for you—and that means living free from unforgiveness. The question you need to answer is this: Will you continue to work *with* God and hasten the work of forgiveness? Or will you dig in where you are stuck right now and refuse to grow deeper into forgiveness? The choice is yours.

Are You Mad at You?

Perhaps, if you feel stuck in unforgiveness, the root of the problem may be that you haven't yet forgiven *yourself.* There is no question that this has been my greatest challenge. The verses above are just a few of the many to which I have turned time and again to renew my mind about how God sees me. My screen saver on my computer reads: "Good Morning! You were washed, but you were sanctified, but you were justified in the name of the Lord Jesus Christ and in the Spirit of our God" (1 Cor. 6:11). I affirm that truth in my life over and over and over. To be honest, I still deal with self-condemnation in some respects. I know the Lord says,

"Therefore there is now no condemnation for those who are in Christ Jesus" (Rom 8:1), but I also know I have an enemy who loves to whisper condemnation in my ear. If I am tired, I am particularly vulnerable to his attacks because he knows I am weak. He loves to strike when our defenses are down. It takes vigilance to resist his attacks. Sometimes I get so tired of the fight. But I know freedom is my goal, and even the fight glorifies God.

As my Father, God is thrilled to see me persisting in my efforts to become truly free from resentment and bitterness toward others and deal with my feelings of abandonment as a child. But He also wants me to be free of the self-loathing that can so quickly seep into my thinking if I am not vigilant. I remind myself constantly that God sees me through Jesus's righteousness. I have committed to forgiving myself at all costs so that I can be truly free of the burden He doesn't want me to bear.

When we are hurt by the consequences of our own sin and choices, we have to forgive ourselves. We discussed briefly in chapter 6 that, theologically, we do not have the authority to forgive ourselves. It is God who must forgive us. But He already has! Forgiving ourselves really means to come to a place of acceptance of our standing before God—seeing ourselves as God sees us.

You can begin by confessing your sin to God. Pray, and be specific. You've just got to own your stuff and say, "I am a flawed person. I am a sinner. But God forgives me, so I can forgive myself." And then, afterward, the enemy is going to come after you. He hates losing ground. Just remember that God is greater than the enemy, and the Holy Spirit living within us gives us His power.

Seeing ourselves as forgiven can be so hard to do when we fail so miserably. As you know by now, more than once I sinned and could not make excuses for my choices or behavior. I had only myself to blame. I felt my failure was too great. I punished myself. I felt unworthy. I hadn't measured up. I felt like I was a disappointment not only to God but to my whole family. Such thinking is focused on God's standards of righteousness as expressed in the Old Testament rather than His total forgiveness and acceptance through Jesus. How easy to see ourselves as the prodigal who deserves nothing more than to feed the swine. But God sees us as His beloved child and comes running toward us to welcome us home and restore to us the full rights and privileges of being His child. My problem was that my sense of guilt and shame were out of proportion to my sense of God's love and grace. Forgiving myself restored that balance of grace, outweighing my sin.

I've also had to recognize *by faith, not by feelings,* that God has forgiven me. If God forgives me, then who am I not to forgive myself? If God forgives you, then who are you not to forgive yourself? You and I must constantly reaffirm our trust in the truth of God's Word, not trust in our feelings. The truth is in 1 John 1:9, "If we confess our sins, He is faithful and righteous to forgive us our sins and to cleanse us from all unrighteousness." My problem, I realized, was not one of *being* forgiven but of *feeling* forgiven. I had to take forgiveness by faith.

Finally, I've had to realize the destructive influence of negative self-talk. I think of negative self-talk like I think of mosquitoes. They are a horrible nuisance in the summer, taking pleasure away from being out of doors. I feel justified when I am able to hit one and see the small smear of blood on my skin. But these days, with threats such as the Zika virus, mosquitoes are far more than a nuisance. They can be deadly. And in many parts of the world, malaria spread by mosquitoes is still a deadly foe. So too is our negative self-talk. It is not just a nuisance. It carries the danger of harming me in fundamental ways—undermining who I am, damaging my self-confidence, hurting my relationships. It even damages my relationship with God, because when I engage in negative self-talk, I am contradicting what God has said about me. It buzzes around in my mind, I swat at it but it comes back. Relentless. It becomes a habit. How easy it is to feel helpless against negative self-talk. Can we not master it? How can we swat it effectively? Sometimes it seems an inevitable consequence of living in a fallen world with an enemy who is always seeking to bring us down to his level. Or is it?

I am a work in progress in this area. I freely admit it. But I am seeing progress! I battle negative thoughts even now, but the point is, I am *engaged* in battle. And I refuse to surrender.

Now is when we must revisit the critical importance of taking every thought captive and renewing our minds. Here is where the analogy of mosquitoes can be a helpful tool.

Prevention

Just as we can use insect repellent to ward off those pesky insects, so too we can use the Word of God to ward off negative self-talk. Nothing is as effective as filling our minds daily with God's truth from the Bible. (I know I have repeated this idea often in this book; I cannot overstate the importance of

God's Word in our daily living. It is important to be in the Word every day. Maybe just a word or phrase or verse, if you have no time for more. But make it a priority. I recommend you journal what you are thinking, then apply the Scripture to it.) This reinforces who we are in Christ and helps us avoid falling into the trap of negative thoughts about ourselves to begin with.

Attack

When we are hit by thoughts of shame and unworthiness, and other self-defeating thoughts, we must immediately take those thoughts captive rather than allowing them to capture us. We can swat them with the truth of God's Word right on the spot and not allow our thoughts to be carried away. We can get control of them and not let them fester and lead to greater sin.

Praise and Thanksgiving

Praising the Lord is a key to silencing all the negative thoughts. Praise and negative thoughts cannot be in the same brain. Praise is thanking God for who He is. Thanksgiving is thanking Him for what He has done. Make it a daily practice—even if it's hard.

Psalm 8:1–2 in *The Message* says,

> God, brilliant Lord,
>> yours is a household name.
> Nursing infants gurgle choruses about you;
>> toddlers shout the songs
> That drown out enemy talk,
>> and silence atheist babble.

Praise is a powerful tool. If you cannot think of what to say in praise, open the psalms anywhere—to any chapter. One of my favorites, which has been a mainstay in my life, is Psalm 40. Pick out your own. Write it in your journal. Pray it to God. Use it.

Healing

After we've been bitten, we must tend to our wounds promptly. A little anti-itch cream goes a long way to keep us from the scratching that can lead to infection. In the same way we can renew our minds by going back to the Word very deliberately, identifying the lie from the enemy and looking up verses to expose that lie and replace it with truth. This final step is important. Too often, even if we are aware, we think, *Oh, I'll just move on. I'm going to ignore those thoughts.* But they can't be ignored. They do the damage even if we're not paying attention to them. We must replace them with the truth about who we are. Battling negative self-talk takes diligence. Self-control. Grit. Determination. But the rewards are worth it. I believe it helps to recall what Jesus answered when He was asked, "Which is the greatest commandment?"

> And He said to him, "'You shall love the Lord your God with all your heart, and with all your soul, and with all your mind.' This is the great and foremost commandment. The second is like it, 'You shall love your neighbor as yourself.'" (Matt. 22:37–39)

So love yourself. Be kind to yourself. This is what Jesus wants for you. This is how to continually forgive yourself.

A Word about Regret, Remorse, and Confession

Of course, when we do sin and the Holy Spirit convicts us of that sin, we are not to mistake that conviction for negative self-talk. It would help here to distinguish between remorse and regret. We all know what regret feels like. *Boy! I wish I hadn't done that.* It involves some feelings of guilt, shame, and unhappiness. We regret the hurt we caused ourselves and others and what it cost us. Regret is self-focused. Regret is miserable.

Remorse does share many of the same feelings, such as guilt and unhappiness. Like regret, it means, *I feel bad about what I did.* But it goes beyond that. Remorse is deeper than regret. It involves *repentance*, which requires sorrow and truth-telling. Remorse takes responsibility for the action. It is not only sorry for hurting another person or sinning against God but involves empathy for the pain caused to the other person. Remorse leads to confession, asking for forgiveness from the offended party, and a true effort not to do it again.

Are You Mad at God?

Above I wrote that, perhaps, if you feel stuck in unforgiveness, the root of the problem may be that you haven't yet forgiven *yourself*. There is another possibility that we should consider. This too is an area where I struggled. *Perhaps you are angry at God.*

I mentioned in the previous chapter that it was during the aftermath of my fourth husband's decision to divorce me that I finally realized my core issue was abandonment. I traced the origin of that sense of abandonment back to childhood.

But I knew there was another area that troubled me. One that was so hard to wrap my brain around: I felt abandoned by God. I felt guilty for even having such thoughts, but I had to face them to have any hope of healing.

The first time I ever really became aware of struggling with anger at God was after my first husband's infidelity. After all, I reasoned, I loved God and was a faithful wife, a leader in my church, a loving mother. Surely, didn't that mean God would take care of me? Why had He allowed my husband to be unfaithful? Why hadn't God prevented this? Why didn't He stop it before it started—or, at least, convict my husband at the first infidelity so he would have immediately repented? Why hadn't He intervened? He could have stopped it but didn't. Why had God allowed it to go on for years?

And then, once I knew of my husband's unfaithfulness and forgave him, why didn't God restore our marriage? For three long years I struggled for restoration and healing, only to have it end in divorce. I distinctly remember claiming the promise of the prophet Haggai, when he said, "'The latter glory of this house will be greater than the former,' says the LORD of hosts, 'and in this place I will give peace'" (Hag. 2:9). I know that promise was made to Israel, but I claimed it personally. I thought my marriage was going to get better, and we would be at peace. I also claimed the promise, "Behold, I am making all things new" (Rev. 21:5). I thought God was going to make my marriage like new. But He didn't.

I got mad at God. I felt He'd let me down. I knew in my head that wasn't the truth, but why wasn't He acting on my behalf? Why didn't He fulfill those promises? For a while

I even gave up. Why was I bothering to read my Bible and pray? It didn't seem to make much difference. The hope I had placed in those promises mocked me. When I was hurting so badly, crying myself to sleep night after night, where was God? Did this mean God didn't care about me? Did this mean God had abandoned me? I cried out to Him but only heard silence. To me, that proved He abandoned me. He was busy with others. I was too insignificant to be bothered with. My spiritual crisis was real and profound. I felt truly lost. Why didn't He answer in a way I could understand?

Yet I belonged to Him. I knew that. His Son had died for me. I believed that. I was at war with myself over my anger at God. After all, I was an evangelical—everything was supposed to be buttoned up, tied down, tucked in. Neat. At first, I had no one to talk to about it, until I finally got help from my pastor and counselor.

I remember coming to a point where I felt I needed to forgive God. Yes, you read that correctly. *Forgive God.* How could I do that? Of course, theologically, there is no such act—to forgive God. But emotionally and psychologically I felt there must be.

I came to understand that I was angry God didn't behave *as I expected Him to.* He didn't fulfill the promises *as I thought He would.* It wasn't God who had failed me. My expectations were wrong. My anger was misplaced. I actually needed to confess my lack of trust in Him when life didn't go my way. In the painful times of my life, I realized, God invites me to trust Him in a larger way.

But experience would teach me that once doesn't do it. Trusting God is a lifelong process.

Now that I've come to recognize my core issue of abandonment and have made some progress in my healing from that old wound, I believe I have a new perspective when my expectations of God are not met. When we have been hurt, we may become angry with God that our journey is so difficult. We tend to think that once we have dealt with our sin, and dealt honestly with ourselves and others, life will get much easier. But it doesn't. Often it gets harder. Rather than get discouraged and angry with God, blaming Him for the wounds we suffer, the broken places in our hearts, and the disappointments we encounter, we are given the privilege of calling out to Him in our distress and asking Him to increase our trust. He waits with a loving heart for us to cry out to Him.

We can confess our anger, bitterness, and resentment of Him and do exactly what Jesus did at Gethsemane—pour out our raw emotions, then relinquish our own will and choose His instead.

Recently I had surgery. It didn't go well. There were complications. I was in a great deal of pain. I couldn't think. I couldn't pray. Finally, I groaned, "Father, I am Your daughter. I need Your help." I just released it all to Him, and a certain peace followed. The pain continued for days longer, but I was calm.

I think that is what God really wants from us. That abandoning trust.

One of the reasons I love the psalms is that in them David expressed his emotions so powerfully, yet after he vented, he always returned to worshiping God. A perfect example is Psalm 55. I recommend you read it now.

Are you angry with God today about something that happened to you? Or something that hasn't happened that you were expecting or for which you were hoping? Turn to the psalms and pray with David to vent your emotions and give voice to your anger so that you can get a new perspective and worship the God who loves you.

Stuck at the What Ifs

We've discussed forgiving yourself. We've discussed forgiving God. Who is it, then, that you still can't forgive? You may be lost among the "what ifs."

What if the person I haven't forgiven has died or is unreachable?

Remember, forgiveness isn't dependent on the other person. It is an act of your will, a decision that you make. It means relinquishing your perceived right to get even. You can do that now. Begin by determining that you will be a forgiving person. Take the first step by praying that God's will be done. You know His will is that you forgive. You have now begun the *process* of forgiveness!

What if the person is not safe?

Remember, forgiveness is not the same as reconciliation. Forgiving doesn't mean trusting the other person, it means wanting the best for them. Can you pray for God's best for that person? Then do it and begin to know the release of forgiveness. It may feel fake at first. Maybe here we could say, "Fake it till you make it." Each effort you make is seen by God and will be honored by God.

What if I asked forgiveness of someone but they wouldn't grant it?

Remember, you are not responsible for the decisions that another person makes. You are responsible for the decisions you make. Did you confess your sin to God and to that person? Did you repent by turning away from your sinful behavior? Now allow God to work in that person's heart in His perfect timing. In the meantime, take your thoughts captive and renew your mind in God's Word; you are forgiven.

I met a young man whom I'll call Blake. Blake's father died when he was a young boy. For years Blake struggled with resentment toward his uncle for not stepping in and doing more to father him in his father's absence. After years of this resentment, Blake was convicted of it by the Holy Spirit. He knew the Spirit was calling him to go ask forgiveness of his uncle. Finally, he got up his nerve and went to see his uncle. "Uncle Jim," he confessed, "for years, since my father's death, I've blamed you for not playing a different role in my life. I have resented you. I've been bitter toward you. I just want to ask your forgiveness."

Uncle Jim didn't say a word. Just awkward silence. Finally, Blake said his goodbyes and left.

Blake did the right thing in going to his uncle, confessing, and asking forgiveness. It is not easy to humble ourselves and ask for forgiveness. It can feel like standing naked before them. Blake also had to come to terms with the reality that he couldn't get from Jim what he didn't have in him to give. Jim evidently didn't have the capacity or inclination to respond to Blake's request for forgiveness. We don't always get the result we hope for, but seeking forgiveness isn't ultimately about our feelings. It is about being obedient to God. Blake could now have a clear conscience.

I once had a very close relationship with a friend. Over time we drifted apart, and I felt responsible for allowing that to happen. I felt that I'd been negligent in our relationship and needed to ask her forgiveness. I went to her and confessed. I told her how much I missed my relationship with her. And I wept. She just sat there. Later I learned she shared that conversation with someone else and ended by saying, "But the relationship will never be the same." Those are the kinds of responses you might get. And it's tough. Seeking to restore a relationship through confession and forgiveness is not an act for the cowardly. It takes a certain amount of bravery to do it. But even more than that, it takes total reliance on God. But it's worth it!

What if my emotions are in the way and I don't feel forgiving?

You are not alone in this challenge! David provides exactly the model we need. How can we forgive the person who wounded us (or someone we love) so deeply? We don't want to. We want to cut that person from our lives forever or just ignore them or forget them. But we can't seem to get them out of our hearts and minds. In our quiet moments, we remember what they did. We review what happened and think about all the biting and hurtful things we could say to them. Maybe we could make them hurt as much they hurt us. Have you had wonderful conversations with yourself in the shower where you cut that person down to size? Where you tell them exactly what you think about them? Welcome to the club.

David knew that feeling too. When I am upset with someone, I love to read Psalm 109 in *The Message* version of the Bible. In it, David tears his enemies up one side and down the other. He calls them a pack of dogs out to get him for no reason. He asks God to send Satan to judge his enemy and pronounce him guilty. David asks that his life be short, his job given to someone else, his wife become a widow, and his children become street urchins. He asks that the bank foreclose on him and wipe him out and no one be there to help him. He asks that his enemy's family tree be cut down. He wants his enemy's parents' sins to be remembered and be recorded in heaven forever. And David goes on, asking God to do terrible things to his enemy. David is over-the-top angry and vengeful. Actually, if you read this psalm in *The Message*, it is nearly comical because David is so full of retribution. He is asking God to do to his enemy all the horrible things he can think of—the very worst. Even asking that his curses be made into a suit of clothes for him to wear every day of the week, and that he bathe in his curses. David was angry. Boy, was he angry!

David was venting his emotions to God. That is the safest place to vent. God can handle that kind of fury. He's bigger than our anger. He's heard everything before, so He isn't shocked or disappointed. It's best to tell God about your anger rather than vent to the one who hurt you or lash out at those closest to you. David knew the only help he had for this situation was in God. And like Jesus in the Garden of Gethsemane, he spilled his emotions in prayer so that he didn't have to take revenge and could forgive.

In Psalm 18, we have a beautiful picture of God coming to the aid of His hurting child. Here David acknowledges that God is his refuge and help. David describes how he was about to go under. He was terrified. He had reached his limit. He called out to God for help. I have this picture of a wounded, broken man about to give up in defeat, at the end of his rope. With a last gasp, he pleaded for help to his Almighty God. This pain-filled cry, though barely audible, echoed down the corridors of heaven to the throne room and rose to God's very own ears.

God heard and gathered Himself up and moved. The earth shook and the heavens rumbled. Smoke came from His nostrils and fire out of His mouth. God came down. Darkness was under His feet, and He rode on the mighty wind. Darkness hid Him like a canopy. Thick clouds covered His dazzling presence. His voice thundered as lightning shot out of the sky; the very foundation of the earth was exposed. Yes. God came down at the sound of His child's whimper. God bent low to scoop up His hurting child, to rescue him, deliver him, and take him out of deep waters, away from the enemy who was too strong for David to battle.

What a great, dramatic image of God coming to David's rescue. David said, "[God] rescued me, because He delighted in me" (Ps. 18:19). God comes to your aid as well. Call on Him to help you forgive. Then pick up and move on.

Emotions aren't bad, they just are. We do feel those feelings. We do have those thoughts. But we also have the tools to deal with them. We can submit them to the Holy Spirit. We can take them to Jesus. We can apply the Word to them. And little by little, they do disappear. Of course, they may show up again. But you can say, "Oh! That's old news. I know exactly what this is. I recognize that tired old train of thought, and I have no intention of climbing aboard. That train hits a dead end."

What if they are not sorry or are a repeat offender?

The person who wounds you time and again is definitely a challenge. They do the same thing repeatedly and leave you deeply hurt, questioning your own value. That is hard to forgive. Some might say it is impossible. The easiest thing, perhaps, is just to cut them out of your life, but that isn't forgiveness. Remember, forgiveness doesn't depend on the other person at all. We forgive out of obedience to God by the power of the Holy Spirit and leave the results to Him. We have done our homework—giving grace, living in grace. Your job is to relinquish the right to make the person pay. Then look for ways to protect yourself in the future and seek God's wisdom to do so. Reconciliation in these cases can be unwise or unsafe. You may want to seek the help of a counselor or mature believer.

"What ifs" aren't the place to get stuck. They are the place to get moving! Think about it. If forgiveness is a way of tapping into the character of God, as we discussed in chapter 4, what is unforgiveness? *Unforgiveness is denying the power of God. It's a lack of trust.* Trust in what? God's ability. Unforgiveness is nearsightedness that sees only what is right here, right now, rather than having an eternal perspective. Unforgiveness is also self-focused. It's the antithesis of the character of God. Forgiveness is God-focused—it is participating in the character of God.

David Stopped Where He Was Stuck

In one aspect of David's life, we see what occurs when forgiveness doesn't happen. This story is an illustration of ruined relationships, ruined lives, bitterness, and tragic things that happen to people who dig in their heels rather than confront, tell themselves the truth, and freely forgive.

David's son Amnon couldn't stop thinking about his half-sister Tamar. She was so beautiful. Every time they crossed paths in the palace, he would turn to look at her, gazing upon her with lust. As the firstborn son of King David, very little was kept from him. Whatever he wanted, all he had to do was ask (or demand), and his desire was fulfilled. This particular desire ate at him like nothing else. Morning after morning he woke, hoping the spell this woman had over him had broken. Instead, the thoughts about her grew each day until they made him sick with desire.

One morning, his cousin Jonadab came to Amnon's chamber and asked, "What's the trouble? Why should the son of a king look so dejected morning after morning?" Amnon put his hands over his face and cried out, "I am in love with Tamar, my brother Absalom's sister" (2 Sam. 13:4 NLT).

Jonadab leaned forward and said, "Look. Here's what you do. You pretend to be sick. When your father comes to check on you, tell him you want Tamar to come make some of your favorite food for you here in your chambers and feed it to you" (see v. 5).

Amnon decided to implement Jonadab's crafty suggestion. He laid down on his bed and pretended to be sick. Sure enough, his father the king came to visit, and Amnon made his request: "I would like my sister Tamar to come care for me. She can make me her special bread. It's the only thing that I could eat right now" (see v. 6).

King David didn't hesitate. He called for Tamar and asked her to go nurse her brother back to health.

When Tamar arrived, she began to make his favorite bread as he watched. But he refused to eat it. "Send everyone out of here," he said. When they had gone, he asked Tamar to bring the food to him in his bedroom. She obeyed. When she approached his bed with the bread, he grabbed her and said, "Come to bed with me, my sister" (v. 11 NIV).

Scripture then tells us she cried out, "No, my brother! . . . Don't force me! Such a thing should not be done in Israel! Don't do this wicked thing" (v. 12 NIV).

She then appealed to him, hoping he cared about *her*.

"What about me? Where could I get rid of my disgrace? And what about you? You would be like one of the wicked fools in Israel. Please speak to the king; he will not keep me from being married to you." But he refused to listen to her, and since he was stronger than she, he raped her. (vv. 13–14 NIV)

Whatever Amnon thought he would feel after he fulfilled his desire—relief, satisfaction, love—I don't suppose he expected the outpouring of emotion he did have. For now he hated her with an intense hatred that was so strong, Scripture says that

In fact, he hated her more than he had loved her. Amnon said to her, "Get up and get out!"

"No!" she said to him. "Sending me away would be a greater wrong than what you have already done to me."

But he refused to listen to her. (vv. 15–16 NIV)

Then Amnon forcefully sent her away. In Tamar's distress, she ripped the sleeves off her robe and put ashes on her head.

225

This is how her brother Absalom understood what happened and brought her to live with him.

Rape is such a violation, heaping shame upon a woman's heart and spirit. Women are often advised to keep quiet, move on, pretend it didn't happen—and this is exactly what Absalom advised his ruined sister to do—to keep quiet and not "take this matter to heart" (v. 20). Like so many victims, she paid for the consequences of her attacker's decisions. She was stripped of her entire future as a wife and mother (as well as her dignity), and lived "in her brother Absalom's house, a desolate [ruined] woman" (v. 20 NIV).

That could have been the end of the story, but it's not. The tentacles of choices and consequences have only just begun to silently slither and grow.

The Bible tells us that Absalom never confronted his brother. Never said anything good or bad to him. He just stopped speaking to him. But he hated him. He nursed the hatred in his heart. He bided his time. King David was furious about what happened—but he did nothing either, also choosing to avoid confrontation.

Mosaic law specified that when a woman was raped, if the man didn't marry her, he was to be stoned. Yet two years pass and justice according to the law had not yet been meted out. We don't know why. But we do know that during those two years, the brothers never spoke—and that couldn't have gone unnoticed.

And what of King David? Did he hope that the turmoil between his children would just go away? Did he hope that everyone would eventually forgive, and that would solve the problem of Amnon's attack? We don't know his heart. We only know that he simply avoided addressing the horrible wrong.

Was Amnon smug and thrilled in his escape of any consequences for his actions? Or did he presume amnesty was his because he was the son of the king and heir to the throne? Or perhaps he had seen his own father lust after a woman named Bathsheba and was simply following his father's lead?

Maybe Absalom kept quiet because he was waiting to see if his father would step up and pronounce justice even though it involved his firstborn son?

When David took no action, Absalom came up with his own plan. He invited his father and all his brothers—except one—to a sheep-shearing party. His father graciously declined, and Absalom asked if Amnon could come in his place. King David seemed a little confused at the request, and asked, "Why should he go with you?" (v. 26 NIV), probably because he knew the two brothers were not speaking and were at odds with each other. However, he gave his consent. Perhaps he was hoping the brothers would repair the rift and all would be well.

But Absalom's plan was to finally mete out justice. Before the party, he told his men to wait until Amnon got drunk and then kill him. You'd think Amnon might've been a little bit suspicious. Perhaps Absalom clapped him on the back and welcomed him as he did his other brothers. And his plan went as he had hoped. Amnon got drunk. Then Absalom's men killed him.

When Jonadab, the cousin who'd helped Amnon plan the rape, told King David about the killing of Amnon, he said, "This has been Absalom's express intention ever since the day Amnon raped his sister Tamar" (v. 32 NIV).

Absalom didn't hang around to see what the consequences would be but fled to the home of his grandfather, the king of Geshur, where he stayed for three years.

Things buried tend to fester and eventually cause far-reaching devastation. Absalom's resentment, bitterness, and anger fomented until they boiled over. Perhaps the incident was forgotten by most or, at the least, people thought all had been resolved between the brothers. It wasn't talked about. It was buried. Alive. It was easier to say nothing, pretend everything was normal. Ignoring it, hoping it would go away. But it didn't. There was no repentance. No forgiveness. And dysfunction reigned!

Had David confronted Amnon about the rape of Tamar, had a punishment been enacted, would this have happened? Would Absalom have orchestrated Amnon's murder? Would David have been left mourning his firstborn son? Would he be estranged from Absalom? I think not. There were many opportunities where choices could have been made—by David and Absalom—that would have turned it around. But both men stopped where they were stuck and tragedy followed.

Don't Stop Where You're Stuck

Today, you and I have choices to make. Do we stop where we are stuck and live in avoidance and unforgiveness? Or do we step up to the challenge to forgive and press forward into forgiveness even when we think we can't?

> Will you keep working at the stain of unforgiveness lurking in your heart, determined to persevere until it's gone?
>
> Will you dwell in the truth that God is not mad at you but has forgiven you of every sin?

Will you forgive yourself by confessing your own sin and then seeing yourself as God sees you?

Will you fight your negative self-talk that seeps into your thinking and distorts your view of yourself as a forgiven and beloved child of God?

Will you replace self-focused regret with God-centered remorse and confession so as to keep a clear conscience?

Will you "forgive God" by surrendering your expectations of how you think God should act and instead trust Him and His decisions?

Will you move forward through the "what ifs" that threaten to stall you out on your pathway toward forgiveness and press on to take hold of the forgiveness that is God's will for you?

Remember that forgiveness is the opportunity to participate in the character of God. Will you participate?

THIRTEEN

Displaying the Character of God

A forgiving spirit is home to humility, divine grace, and love, which give witness to a life dedicated to God and filled with God's presence.

J. Randall O'Brien

Does forgiveness really create a lasting transformation? Is that a realistic hope? Does it heal the brokenness? Restore relationships? In a word—yes!

I'm not claiming that things will always be as they were before the wrong took place. Wounds heal into scars, and often scars do not disappear. We may be forever marked in those broken places. But when we are all about displaying the character of God, He uses these once-broken places in our lives for His glory. He transforms them into symbols of the love and sacrifice of Jesus for the forgiveness of our sins—like the scars on His hands and His feet and His side.

I can look at my life now and see all the broken places God has transformed for His use and my joy. I would never have thought it possible when I was going through the deep valley of depression and divorce. More than once I was sure my life was in shambles, never to be used again. But I remember telling God, "If You can use this mess, You are welcome to it." He heard that short prayer and, over time, transformed my deep pain and hurtful experiences into something that helps others. It gives Him great joy to take that which was broken and make it useful. Not only useful but perfect for His purpose.

I don't know *how* He does it; I only know He *does*. He did it for me.

Brokenness is important. It binds us to our fellow humans— we are all broken in some way. Too often, we think we are the only one. After I gave my brief testimony at my father's funeral, so many came up to me to tell me how meaningful it was to them—that it helped them realize they weren't alone. Brokenness is everywhere. It does not disqualify us from God's use. It qualifies us!

God is in the transformation business and truly did transform my mess and make it my message. When we are in pain, when we cannot see any possible good that can come out of it, how easy to think we are the only one. But God transforms our brokenness by His wonderful grace through forgiveness so we do not have to stay broken. Not that we are made perfect while yet on this earth. More like we have been recycled. Repurposed for His use.

We never know what blessings will unfold when we decide to intentionally dedicate ourselves to following God's ways of forgiveness.

When I visited Angola Prison and met Michael on death row, I was no stranger to the ways of God. I'd been walking in faith all my life. At that point however, I was in my fourth marriage, and you now know to some extent the pain and turmoil I was experiencing, the patterns I'd not yet broken free of, the struggle I was having to forgive myself, "forgive God," (by which I mean coming to terms with my unmet expectations of what I'd expected God to do), and forgive my father. When I visited with Michael, I saw freedom in his eyes and heard that same freedom in his voice as he sang the words, "It is well with my soul." It was a freedom I wanted.

It is a freedom I now have!

I can't point to one particular moment that was the turning point. All I can say is that in prayerfully wrestling through all the concepts I've presented in this book, in finally coming to terms with forgiving my father, forgiving myself, and forgiving God, I stepped over a threshold and into a grace-filled space in my spirit where forgiveness reigns. The burdens of unforgiveness are gone. I've never known a freedom quite like it.

I will, no doubt, be tested yet in the future. I will hurt someone, however unintentionally, and will need to humble myself and ask forgiveness. I will be hurt again and will need to offer forgiveness. And surely, I will disappoint myself again and need to continually practice forgiving myself. We do, after all, live in a fallen world, and I know that as God "completes" His work in me, He still has so much work to do. Like the onion, there are more layers to come.

But I also know I have the tools I need to walk in forgiveness, and I've found a closeness to Jesus when I do. His words as He was being nailed to the cross echo in my heart. *Father, forgive them, for they know not what they do.* Forgiveness is the great equalizer among those called by His name—every one of us would stand condemned if not for the eternal forgiveness given so generously by our Savior, who willingly poured His blood out for us. How can we do less than forgive one another? The more clearly we recognize how short we all fall, the more clearly we see the extent and power of God's grace and want to share it with one another. That said, I don't ever want to give the impression that asking for or giving forgiveness is easy.

Forgiveness isn't the easy way. It is the Savior's way.

Unfinished Business

Some years ago, I had a very close friendship with a woman I'll call Doris. We were closer than sisters. We talked every day and prayed together once a week, maybe more. Our families were frequently together for holidays and vacations. As couples, we enjoyed teasing and playing jokes on each other. There was nothing Doris and I couldn't say to one another, and we confided our darkest secrets to each other. She was a dear, dear friend.

One day her husband confided in me that he was having an emotional affair. I didn't know what to do with that. I wanted to help him. I listened to him and prayed with him several times. But I didn't know what else to do, so, like King David in the previous chapter, I did nothing. Sadly, I then withdrew from them both. What a loss.

Eventually Doris's husband's emotional affair and the fact that he had confided in me all came to light. Doris was deeply wounded that I had not told her about her husband's inappropriate relationship. Shortly thereafter, they moved across the country. But they were not gone from my heart and mind. I missed them.

For many years the brokenness of our relationship nagged at me. What could I have done differently? What could I do to heal the relationship? Should I just stuff down my memories and feelings and forget them? But I couldn't move on. As a couple, they were so very dear to me. They had seen me through the rough waters when my first husband's infidelity was revealed and in the aftermath with the divorce. I felt that in my silence I had betrayed her, my sweetest, closest friend. It was unfinished business. I was wrong and I couldn't "move on" until I addressed it in some manner with her.

There came a time when I was scheduled to speak in their city, so I let them know I was coming and asked if they would join me for dinner one evening. I knew God was giving me an opportunity to begin to address with them what I had done. But if I brought it up, would they use this opportunity to unload all their hurt and anger on me? Would they reject my effort? I was anxious as I waited to greet them.

They were both very gracious and picked me up at my hotel and took me to one of their favorite eateries. We ordered, and as we sat outside on a lovely evening under the starry sky we talked of our children and caught up on our lives, all while ignoring the elephant in the room. Finally, with a prayer in my heart, I told them I was there to ask their forgiveness. I told them how sorry I was and asked them to forgive me.

Her eyes teared up. He ordered another drink! Then, yes, they forgave me. I realized, however, that we'd have to walk it out in the months and years to come. The door was now open for a new, healthy friendship, even though it would take time.

I have seen them a number of times in subsequent years and I sense in them, and in me, a relaxing warmth. We are able to laugh and talk about the "joys" of growing older. The three of us have moved on in good ways. I miss the relationship I had with Doris, but it could never be the same—nor should it be. We are different people than we were then, and I know we grew through the experience we had together.

What if I hadn't invited them for dinner? What if I had just glossed over it, ignoring what I knew I had done wrong? What if I had not asked for forgiveness? Would fire fall from heaven? Would God get mad at me? No. But God wants me to be free of those things that keep me bound in shame and fear. He wants me to experience the freedom of restored relationships. He wants me transformed from self-focused to God-focused. He wants good things for me. He didn't get me into the mess. I did that myself. But He gave me a pathway out of the mess—the pathway of forgiveness. It was my choice to take that pathway or not. I am grateful I did. It was scary. We don't want to be rejected or make ourselves vulnerable, but I have found when He puts something in our hearts, He is usually preparing the way, and He will give us the opportunity.

God Displays His Character through Joseph

Of all the remarkable stories told in the Bible, there is one story of forgiveness that holds a special place in my heart. It is a story that gives great insights and inspires me to persevere in forgiveness. It is the story of Joseph. I'd like to give you an assignment as you read through my telling of it. Imagine what you would have done if you were Joseph. What would your reactions have been? Think about the struggles you may have had if you were in Joseph's place—both in forgiving others and forgiving God. What light does the ending of the story shed on those struggles?

Joseph appears to me to be an almost perfect person in the Bible. He seemed to do everything right. He made wise and godly choices even when he was far away from home, unfairly accused and imprisoned, and under intense pressure.

However, he seemed to start out as a bratty teenager! He was his father's favorite, and his father made no bones about it. "Now Israel [Jacob] loved Joseph more than all his sons, because he was the son of his old age; and he made him a varicolored tunic" (Gen. 37:3). As we saw in the stories of Jacob and Esau, favoritism in a family is divisive and destructive to the family unit. It creates competition and jealousy. In this case, Joseph didn't help matters any. As he tended sheep with his brothers, he would wear that fancy tunic. Was he flaunting his father's partiality? And then he tattled on them to their father. Is it any surprise that they were jealous of him and that "They hated him and could not speak to him on friendly terms" (v. 4)?

Joseph couldn't leave it there. He tells his brothers not just one but *two* dreams where he was the hero and they served him. Certainly, Joseph's actions did not endear himself to them. In fact, Scripture says—twice—that "they hated him even more" (vv. 5, 8). Is it any wonder that Joseph's arrogance got under their skin?

One day, Jacob asked Joseph to go check on his brothers, who were away tending the flocks. When his brothers saw him coming in the distance, they plotted to kill him. However, the oldest brother, Reuben, suggested they not kill him or shed his blood, but strip him of his cloak and throw him into a pit. They all agreed.

Clearly, their actions didn't bother them much, for after they threw him into the pit, they sat down to have a meal, completely indifferent to their little brother. As the men ate, they spotted a caravan on the way to sell its wares in Egypt and saw the answer to their problem—they sold Joseph to the traders. To cover their act of treachery, they killed an animal, put its blood on Joseph's special tunic, and showed it to their father, deceiving him. When he examined it, he reached the conclusion that a wild animal had killed Joseph. Brokenhearted, Jacob mourned for a long time, refusing to be comforted.

Can you imagine being sold into slavery by your own family? When they grabbed Joseph to toss him into the pit, he had to be confused, maybe bruised and battered. His brothers sat down to eat right afterward, so he must have been hungry. Was he yelling for help? Crying? Begging them to pull him out? Without his tunic, was he cold? He was alone and scared. And what about their horrible deception of their elderly father? To break his heart like that?

Joseph's jealous brothers belittled him. His own family mistreated and abused him. He went from favored son to just another slave in a foreign country where he didn't know the language or culture. His life wasn't turning out as he expected. From the moment he was thrown into the pit, then betrayed by his own brothers and sold like a trinket, he had time to become very angry and bitter. Did he question God— the God who had revealed Himself dramatically to his father at Bethel and told him, "A nation and a company of nations will come forth from you, and kings shall come forth from you. The land which I gave to Abraham and Isaac, I will give it to you, and I will give the land to your descendants after you" (35:11–12)? Was that promise mocking him? Was the relationship his father had with God just a cruel joke?

His father had no doubt instilled in Joseph a worldview that was centered on the powerful God of Israel. Jacob would have passed on the stories of creation, the fall, the flood. Of Abraham, his great-grandfather, and Sarah, his great-grandmother. The faith they had in *Yahweh*. Of the near-sacrifice of Isaac. And the journey to Canaan with all the miracles and adventures along the way, as well as the promise of a great nation and deliverer yet to come. These would have been Joseph's bedtime stories, instilling in him trust of a great God. Were those stories really true? Did ugly doubts gnaw away at him?

The traders took Joseph to Egypt and sold him to a man named Potiphar, who was Pharaoh's officer and captain of the bodyguard. As Joseph lived in the midst of a pagan culture that worshiped their own gods, he chose to remain faithful to the God of Israel—even when no one was watching. He must have learned well at his father's knee.

The Bible tells us that "The Lord was with Joseph, so he became a successful man" (39:2). He impressed Potiphar so much that Potiphar made Joseph the manager of all he owned. He trusted Joseph implicitly.

It didn't take long for Potiphar's wife to notice this handsome young slave. Day after day she attempted to seduce him. Joseph was far away from home; no one would know if he gave in. But he would have none of it. He considered such a thing a sin against God. She made one last lunge at him and, as he fled her presence, she clutched at his garment, wrenching it off him. But he got away.

She was so angry at Joseph's rejection that she told her husband Joseph attacked her, and she had his garment to prove it. When she told Potiphar her lie, he became angry and put Joseph in prison. He was jailed for doing the right thing. That can make one very bitter—but not Joseph.

The Lord was with Joseph in prison and again gave him favor with the warden. He saw the leadership in Joseph and put him in charge of the other prisoners. The Bible says, "the LORD was with him; and whatever he did, the LORD made to prosper" (v. 23). That's nice, but Joseph was still in prison. He wasn't free to enjoy life as he had dreamed. His life was not what he'd expected it to be—far from it.

Soon Pharaoh's cupbearer and baker made Pharaoh angry, and he threw them both in the prison where Joseph was.

One night they each had a disturbing dream and puzzled over the meanings. When Joseph asked why they looked so unhappy, they told him they had no one to interpret their dreams.

Joseph told them that all interpretation belongs to God. When they relayed their dreams to him, Joseph was able to interpret them. He asked them to remember him when they got out of jail because he was innocent and did not deserve to be there. They agreed and were soon released in celebration of Pharaoh's birthday. But they forgot all about Joseph and their promise to him.

After two years, with Joseph still languishing in prison, Pharaoh himself had two dreams that he did not understand. None of his magicians or wise men knew what they meant. But the cupbearer finally remembered Joseph and told Pharaoh of his experience in jail when Joseph had revealed the meaning of his dream. Pharaoh sent for Joseph and asked him to interpret his dreams. Joseph would take no credit for himself, but boldly told Pharaoh that it was God who gave answers, not him.

Pharaoh listened to all Joseph said, then told him, "Since God has informed you of all this, there is no one so discerning and wise as you are. You shall be over my house, and according to your command all my people shall do homage; only in the throne I will be greater than you. . . . See, I have set you over all the land of Egypt" (41:39–41). So, twenty-three years after Joseph had been sold as a slave by his brothers to the band of traders, he was given the most powerful position in all Egypt—second only to Pharaoh.

Surely during those twenty-three years Joseph must have had moments when he felt totally forgotten, so far from all he had known. Would he ever see his father again? Did his father think of him? How could he handle all the brokenness and unfairness in his life? Yet God had a remarkable plan for Joseph's life, a plan that was hinted at in Joseph's childhood dreams. And soon, they were to come to fulfillment.

He conducted Pharaoh's affairs with wisdom and shrewdness, leading Egypt in their seven years of prosperity to store a percentage of all food production. But as his dream had foretold, seven hard years followed. There was a great famine throughout the whole region, and people came from far and wide to buy grain from Egypt.

News of Egypt's bounty reached Canaan. Jacob's family was also suffering from the famine, so Jacob asked ten of his sons to go to Egypt to buy grain. When they arrived in Egypt, Joseph recognized the Hebrew men instantly, but they did not recognize this powerful man as their annoying, bratty little brother. This was Joseph's chance to get even! He was a ruler second only to Pharaoh, and no one would have questioned him if he had his brothers arrested and thrown into jail to await a painful death. He could do with them what he wished. Had he dreamed about this day—a day of retribution? He could get even now for all the injustice he had suffered. The betrayal. The loneliness. I confess that that is probably what I would have done—or at least thought about. I am sure I would have spent all those years building a big head of steam of bitterness and resentment. How understandable it would have been if Joseph had been ready to blow and spew anger and vitriol all over those brothers and anyone who got in his way.

But that wasn't who Joseph was.

Although Joseph had twenty-three long years to develop resentment and bitterness, he also had twenty-three years to learn to forgive. The Bible doesn't tell us how he forgave—it only shows us the results of forgiveness. He did his homework and was prepared to forgive his brothers in a way that restored him, his family, and his people. Forgiveness has that kind of potential for transformation.

Yes, he was young when he was sold into slavery, but it is clear from Scripture that Joseph stayed true to God and His purpose, though he was surrounded by a pagan culture that worshiped many gods. He stayed true to the God of his father when he refused Potiphar's wife and when he acknowledged God as the interpreter of dreams both to his two fellow prisoners and to Pharaoh himself. He acknowledged God as the source of the answers to the problem of seven years of famine. He was trusting in the God of Abraham and Isaac and Jacob. But it was no longer his father's faith in God—it was his own faith in God. And God honored Joseph for honoring Him. God said, "For those who honor Me I will honor, and those who despise Me will be lightly esteemed" (1 Sam. 2:30).

So, when Joseph's brothers bowed before him, he devised some tests to see what was in their hearts. He accused them of being spies and demanded they bring their youngest brother to Egypt as proof they weren't lying. The brothers agonized over this charge. They had no influence, no status—they were aliens. They were afraid for their lives and could do nothing but obey this man who was all-powerful in Egypt. Their father's fear of losing yet another son played on their minds; their guilty consciences played havoc in their thinking. They argued and pointed fingers among themselves, saying they were being punished for selling Joseph years before. They didn't realize Joseph understood everything they said!

Eventually they convinced their father, Jacob, to send his youngest son, Benjamin, to Egypt with them because Judah guaranteed his safety. When they arrived back in Egypt, Joseph sent them an invitation for dinner that evening. The brothers were afraid he was setting them up to kill them. When they arrived for dinner, the youngest brother was with them. Joseph asked if he was the one they had told him about, and they confirmed it. Then Joseph had everyone but his brothers leave the room because he was overcome with weeping.

When they were alone, he revealed himself to his brothers. They were stunned into silence. He wanted them to come closer. Dr. R. T. Kendall said he made all the Egyptians leave their presence and drew them close because he didn't want any of the Egyptians to overhear what his brothers had done to him by selling him into slavery.[1] What a true sign of forgiveness, that the wounded party did not want everyone to know what these men had done to him. His words to his brothers, rather than being the berating they deserved, were reassuring and kind. "Do not be grieved or angry with yourselves, because you sold me here, for God sent me before you to preserve life . . . it was not you who sent me here, but God" (Gen. 45:5, 8).

Joseph then sent them back to go get his father. Word spread to Pharaoh about Joseph's brothers, and he issued a gracious invitation for the whole family to come live in the land of Egypt and provided abundantly for them. Joseph's forgiveness kept him from bitterness and anger. It transformed the life of his family, his nation, and the geopolitical world of the day.

But it did even more than that. There is another reason that Joseph's story has resonated through the ages. Two reasons, actually.

Making Our Wounds Sacred and Displaying the Character of God

In chapter 4 we explored two transformative principles about forgiveness that set the stage for the subsequent chapters of this book. The first was this: *forgiveness is the opportunity to make our wounds sacred.* I know we've covered a lot of material since then, so let me refresh your memory. I wrote,

Making our wounds sacred has the power to transform them. In the giving of our wounds over to God for His service, we are saying, *Lord, yes, this hurts. But I'm giving it to You for Your use. Transform it into something that reflects You and Your relentless love. Give it a holy purpose that I can see and recognize.* When we dedicate our wounds to God, we know that He won't waste them but will use them for His glory and our good. So then, let's keep our eyes open for the evidence of God's grace and work in the midst of our pain. This will begin to replace the pain with anticipation.

Do you see how Joseph made his wounds sacred? The wounds of being thrown into the pit, of being sold into slavery by his brothers, of being unjustly accused by Potiphar's wife, of serving years in prison for a crime he didn't commit? Twenty-three years of agonizing wounds, not the least of which was being separated from the father he loved and from his own people and land. He turned those wounds over to God for His service, and God used them all to not only save the Egyptians from starvation but to save His chosen people as well. That example inspires me to anticipate how God might use my wounds. There is hope in the pit.

The second principle we explored was this: *when we forgive, we are displaying the character of God.* I wrote,

In the end, we come down to this very simple truth: Jesus said to forgive over and over and over and over again. Forgiveness reflects His nature. That's what He did *for* us. That's what He wants *from* us. That is what He is doing *in* us. And isn't that what we ultimately want?

Forgiveness is a sacred sacrifice you offer to God, a gift you give to Him. It is an opportunity to practice a divine quality.

Let's elevate forgiveness to the realm of the holy. It's about having the opportunity to model and display God's character to a broken world in desperate need of true forgiveness.

Joseph, in his act of forgiving his brothers, displayed God's character not only to his brothers but also to us. He foreshadowed the very character of Jesus—unjustly accused, serving a sentence He did not deserve, yet through His act of sacrifice pouring out rich and undeserved blessings on His people, the very people who had wronged Him. Joseph modeled God's character for all of us to see.

His story makes me want to do the same! I too want to make my wounds sacred through forgiveness. I too want to display God's character to a broken world.

The act of forgiveness is about more, so much more, than our emotional well-being. Therefore, when we forgive, we enter into a very divine grace, a sacred behavior. I finally understand that the act of forgiveness is not about me and my feelings. It is a form of true worship. It is being willing to lay aside my desires for what I think is fair, pick up my cross, and follow after Jesus. It says I'm going to make my decisions not based on what I want, which is revenge; not based on what I feel, which is anger and bitterness, but based instead *on my purpose,* which is to glorify God.

We know from Ephesians 4:32 that we are called to follow the example Jesus has set for us. Let's assume for a moment that the reason for this is not only because Jesus is perfect, and we should strive to be likewise, but because Jesus was really on to something that *helps* us to forgive. Let's look at that verse again: "Be kind to one another, tender-hearted, forgiving each other, just as God in Christ also has forgiven you." If we choose a motivation that is *just as God in Christ* was motivated, then we won't be forgiving for our own sakes, so that we feel better. We will be forgiving in order to display God's character.

Think about it. When Jesus hung dying on the cross, He wasn't thinking about Himself—how He felt and how He would benefit. His words from the cross tell us His thoughts. He was thinking about the well-being of those who were crucifying Him: "Father, forgive them . . ." He was thinking about what He was accomplishing for God: "It is finished." Though He was suffering in agony just like you and I would suffer under those conditions, though He was being brutalized beyond our imagination, He was thinking about the eternal salvation of the thief hanging by His side and of the well-being of His mother standing before Him. Even before Calvary, He was at work preparing His disciples for the crucifixion so that they would see His willingness to suffer and die for our forgiveness as an act of love with His words, "Greater love has no one than this, that one lay down his life for his friends" (John 15:13). Jesus was God-centered and other-centered, not self-centered, even as He bled and died for our forgiveness.

As you consider these two motivations to forgive—to make our wounds sacred and to display the character of God—how do they compare with the motives you've experienced in the past as you confronted the issue of granting forgiveness or asking for forgiveness?

What wounds do you still carry concerning forgiveness? Consider this question: What good might God bring out of your wounds? Are you willing to dedicate your wounds to God and ask Him to accomplish His will through them?

Have you ever before considered how asking forgiveness or giving forgiveness might display God's character through you? How might you grow in God's grace, in experiencing God's presence and blessings? How might your walking in forgiveness affect your spiritual life, your family's lives, or the lives of others you care deeply about? Prayerfully consider how strong your motivation is to walk more closely with God. Are you willing to pray, here and now, that God increase that desire in you?

Take a few minutes now to turn to back to the first page of each chapter of this book. Get a journal and reread the opening quotes. Reconsider the main point of each chapter. By following the guidance of each chapter, you will walk through the process of forgiveness from beginning to end. Write down the names of those God brings to your mind— those who you need to ask forgiveness of or those you need to forgive. Take your time to pray and ask God's Spirit to reveal what you need to know and do.

Write down the new ways you hope to experience God's presence and power in your life. Are you willing to give your wounds to Jesus and ask Him to help you, through forgiveness, grow in reflecting God's power to a hurting, broken world?

As you consider these questions, here is my prayer for you: "Now may the God of hope fill you with all joy and peace in believing, so that you will abound in hope by the power of the Holy Spirit" (Rom. 15:13).

FOURTEEN

Intimacy with God

Forgiveness is not an occasional act, it is a constant attitude.

Martin Luther King Jr.

There is one final story from my life that I feel it is time to tell. It is the story of my relationship with my daughter Windsor. Like Joseph's story, it is a family saga that transpired over many years. I've told bits and pieces of our earlier relationship in previous books, but it wasn't until I was writing this book on forgiveness that the full scope of the role of forgiveness in our story—the transformation in both Windsor and in me—became clear. Naturally, I tell this with her permission.

Windsor was fourteen when my first marriage ended. I watched in agony as her pain unfolded before my eyes. I told much of this in my book *In Every Pew Sits a Broken Heart*. She, like me, felt insecure and "looked for love in all the wrong places." She ended up getting pregnant at age sixteen and decided to release that baby girl into the loving arms of adoptive parents. Then she began a downward spiral that was heartbreaking to watch. She seemed to go from one bad relationship to another. I was desperate to help her. In addition to trying to express my love and doing my best to set protective, healthy boundaries, I bought her a dog to care for and gave her flying lessons, trying in vain to distract her from the young men who were hanging around. I also got her in to see a good counselor.

When she was a senior in high school, I was frantic in my concern for her but was also angry—very angry—that she simply would not obey my rules. Naturally, my anger only fueled the dysfunction. At one point, I was so angry and frustrated—we'd had a big fight—I went upstairs to her room and began throwing her clothes out the window. Not one of my better moments! As I look back now, it must have looked comical from the outside. I lived on a golf course at the time, and now I wonder what the golfers thought as they saw clothing flying out the upstairs windows! But it wasn't funny to me at the time, nor to Windsor. We pushed each other's buttons—all the wrong ones. Finally, I made a "contract" with her about what was expected, setting boundaries and goals. She simply would not cooperate. I told her she could not live in my home and disobey the rules. So she walked out.

I begged her not to go. I knew the kinds of people she was going to be living with. They had no rules, and I feared for her. But she left, slamming the door behind her. I can still hear the thud in my mind. I wept. My heart was broken, truly broken in a way it hadn't been before.

Still, we maintained a relationship—an uneasy one. She would stop by for dinner from time to time but was clearly enjoying her newfound freedom. However, I became aware she was skipping school. I contacted the family she was living with, and they showed no concern even though they were "contributing to the delinquency of a minor" by allowing truancy and therefore were breaking the law.

Windsor's father was attending a conference nearby in Williamsburg. He tried to persuade her to move to Texas to live with him. She would have no part of that. Under the advice of a counselor, her father and I decided we would confront her together. We wanted to make it a surprise and catch the family she was staying with off guard. The police went with us to speak with the adults in that family.

As you can imagine, it was an ugly scene. She fought like a wildcat. A police officer put her in the back of his squad car. She was cursing up a storm. Her father then had to go back to Williamsburg, so I was left to handle the drama the best I could. The officer took her down to the police station. I followed. As soon as I walked into the station, I could hear her. She was making quite a scene. I was a wreck inside but was determined not to show it. This wasn't turning out at all like I'd hoped. How was this helping?

I knew she needed to know I would go to any lengths to rescue her from what I saw as a bad situation getting worse—that she was that important to me. There was no way I was going to leave her at the police station overnight. It was after hours, and I had to find someone to help me. The one official I was finally able to get on the phone brushed me off like I was an "undesirable." Sometime later that evening he came down to the station very apologetically. He'd found out at home that we were Billy Graham's family. (Though I was very grateful he'd come, I found this special treatment very disturbing. It made me hurt for how others must be treated in their dire circumstances.) Now he was willing to assist me in signing all the correct documents that enabled me to take Windsor home that night.

But she didn't stay. She was soon gone again.

My emotions ran the gamut. I loved my daughter and feared for her safety and her future. I berated myself for not knowing how to handle the situation with more wisdom and grace. I was also angry, and though I hate to admit it, I was also embarrassed to be put in such a position publically. It's one thing when your family is having problems but quite another when it is out in the open and overheard by others. I didn't want the world to know. We lived in a small town. There was no place to hide. But Windsor didn't seem to care.

Windsor continued her pursuit of young men and became pregnant again. We got her into a college that was willing to work with her situation. We found a one-bedroom apartment near campus. It was a dreary place but she was determined to make it on her own. The baby arrived at Thanksgiving, and she was resolute about raising this child as a single mother. I drove down to pick Windsor and the baby up for the Christmas holidays, but I did not want to rescue her. She had put herself in this position. I tried my best to be loving but had grave concerns about her ability to care for the baby while doing her schoolwork. The school was wonderful. They bent over backward to help her. And she worked hard—until another boy showed up.

By this time, I was disgusted. Why couldn't she see? Was there something missing in her psyche? I just couldn't figure it out. I refused to get on her roller coaster, for that's what it was—an emotional roller coaster. But time and again I did get sucked in, and we clashed. I tried to set boundaries, but Windsor had a way of pushing hard against them. It was more than difficult. We seemed to always be fighting. It was not working between us at all.

I loved her. I knew she was desperately hurting. I never did see her as rebellious, per se, but rather just wanting to make her pain go away. My heart ached at the hurt she must be carrying. At that point, she became willing to go live with her father for a brief time in Texas. He didn't know how to set or keep boundaries. He tried to be her friend. (I am sure she thought I was trying to be her jailer.) Then the lady Windsor had lived with when she was expecting both babies said she could come back to stay with her in Philadelphia, which she did.

The distance helped, and time passed. Months became years. She found an apartment in a Philadelphia suburb and lived life as a single mother. She got her Realtor's license and her insurance license in order to support herself. I admired her tenacity. We chose to share holidays together. We tried to act normally. But I didn't feel as if I could be close to her. She wasn't a safe place for me, and I'm sure she felt I wasn't a safe place for her.

By this time I had married my third husband. My girls loved him. He and my daughter Noelle were helpful with Windsor. They each had a good relationship with her and more patience than I did. She came to the beach with us for family vacations. I welcomed her but couldn't seem to feel free with her. I felt burned out in our relationship, but I knew she wanted to have a closer relationship with me. This made me sad, and, naturally, I battled with my familiar negative self-talk, which didn't help matters any.

But we never gave up. We were family. There was a bond between us that would not break, for which I am so grateful. We shared a deep caring for other young women who faced unwed pregnancies, and so we chose to write two books together. One was about her pregnancy and the other about the release of her first child for adoption. We both felt that what she had been through would benefit others. There were some tough moments during the writing when she would threaten to pull out of the whole project, but she could see that her story was powerful and could help many others, so she stuck with it. We agreed on that. But not much else.

When my third marriage ended in divorce after almost ten years, I was brokenhearted but I had to move forward. I was so sad for the grief this caused for each of my children, but especially concerned for the effects on Windsor. He had become like a father to her in many ways. I hated being a source of more pain in her life.

A few years later, she married a wonderful man who had a son the same age as her son. Things seemed to stabilize for Windsor and for our relationship. It wasn't long after that I married my fourth husband. Windsor didn't like him at all, and was very vocal about it. All three of my children were against the relationship, as were my two sons-in-law, and the choices I made put a strain on my relationships with them. A year and a half later my husband had his terrible automobile accident and was very badly injured and on life support. Windsor by this time had a special needs child who had spent months in the hospital. She knew her way around medical machines, doctors, and medicines. She came down to Virginia to be an advocate for my husband and me during that time. She was a huge support. Her presence meant everything to me.

While my husband was in rehab, Windsor, Sara (the lady she lived with in Philadelphia), and I were invited to speak at a pro-life event on Prince Edward Island in Canada. Windsor had never spoken in public, but we both agreed that this might be a good time to test the waters. She was nervous and I was nervous for her. The lady spearheading the event was kind and understanding. Sara talked of her experience with helping several unwed mothers through the process, and I introduced Windsor's and my story. Then I introduced Windsor, and she told her story.

I wept throughout Windsor's entire talk. She was poised and effective at connecting with the audience, and she put so much effort into it. Those tears were healing. God did a work in my heart as I listened to my daughter talk about the struggles she had gone through and God's grace in her own life.

My heart opened to her in a new way, and I realized we had truly forgiven each other. I then made some closing remarks. It worked seamlessly.

Not long after that my fourth husband filed for divorce, and once again I was devastated, not only for my own pain but for all I'd put my children through. My children were supportive throughout. But I carried a deep sense of shame and guilt. The Lord impressed on me that I had some important unfinished business. In order to address it, I needed to get my children and their spouses and those grandchildren who were old enough all together.

I prayed about the right timing. The Lord guided me. I waited for Easter Sunday. After all, isn't Easter all about forgiveness?

We gathered as a family after church at Noelle's home, which overlooked the Blue Ridge Mountains. After a nice Easter lunch, we were sitting together on the patio while the younger grandchildren were playing in the yard, and I told them I wanted to talk to them.

"I have something I need to say to all of you," I began. Though I felt a bit nervous, I also felt a sense of supernatural peace. I knew the Lord had led me to this moment, and I was ready for it.

They blanched, thinking that something awful had happened or that I was ill.

Without fanfare, I told them I needed to ask their forgiveness. I realized I had put them through some difficult things and situations. I told them I had been wrong and needed their forgiveness.

Then I went around the circle and, one by one, I asked each of them, including my sons-in-law, "Will you forgive me?"

"Yes, I forgive you," I was told over and over. More than one told me they didn't really think I needed to ask their forgiveness, but I insisted that I did need it.

Then it was Windsor's turn. "Windsor, will you forgive me?" As I asked, I thought back over our unhappy and complicated history. I truly knew I needed her forgiveness.

There was no hesitation from Windsor. "Yes," she answered, her eyes locked on mine.

At that moment a beautiful healing—a restoration—took place in me.

Is it easy to ask for your children's and grandchildren's forgiveness? No. It is humbling. After all, I'm the mom! I'm supposed to have it all together. But obviously, my children *knew* I didn't have it all together. They'd lived through all my bad choices. They'd seen my willfulness and stubbornness. They needed to know we all are in need of forgiveness and grace. I needed to set the example—in a good way this time!

New Intimacy with God

One recent Sunday I was in Sunday school class as we compared the culture of Paul's time with our own. The teacher asked us when we believed our own culture began the downward slide. A man in the back of the room called out, "When we allowed divorce." His comment didn't faze me, but as I thought about it I realized God had indeed set me free!

After class, the gentleman asked to speak to me. "I'm sorry," he said. "What I meant to say was 'easy divorce.'" I assured him I was not hurt, embarrassed, offended, or upset in any way. And I meant it. I had a new freedom from the condemnation I had for so long heaped upon myself. I realized I stood in the reality of, "Therefore there is now no condemnation for those who are in Christ Jesus" (Rom. 8:1). I had experienced this truth in a deep way. Not just in my head but in my spirit as well.

I thought back to the Easter Sunday when I'd asked for my family's forgiveness and experienced the relief and closure they gave me that day. I know that my Easter Sundays will never be the same. I will forever celebrate on that day how the cross of Christ truly did cover all my sins, for the forgiveness granted me by my family made it so real to me.

The cross and the resurrection cover everything we have talked about in this book. Easter calls us out from the grave of unforgiveness into the resurrected life of forgiveness. We die to self and are raised anew to His life in us. That is the miracle of forgiveness!

Through that miracle—both in asking for and freely giving forgiveness—we have the enormous privilege of walking with God in an intimate way. As we discussed earlier, forgiveness is His habit. And when we forgive and ask forgiveness, we walk so closely with God that He inhabits our decision.

The almighty God, Creator of heaven and earth, wants you to participate in His holy character. What a high calling! Experiencing forgiveness is not only freeing but transformative. It goes to our core and reshapes us in His image. God rejoices as His holiness grows in us. He loves us so much He wants us to *enjoy* this experience. He wants us to savor it—to taste what it is to have His character forming in us, working out His purposes in order to show His glory to this broken world.

It is a miraculous gift He wants us to experience—both in receiving and demonstrating for others what it is to be free as we reflect His character.

You don't need to know *how* God's story of forgiveness will play out in your life, only that it *will* when you choose the way of forgiveness! May you, today, experience the miracle of forgiveness.

Acknowledgments

I have been told that acknowledgments go in ascending order—the most valuable first—or is it descending order—the most valuable last? Oh, I don't know. But in the case of this book, it has to be ascending, descending, on the sides, in the middle, over the top—any way you want to arrange it. Hands down, I owe so very much to Cindy Lambert.

Cindy has believed in me from the very beginning—when we were both starting out. She, as an editor for Zondervan, and me, as a fledgling author. We became friends the moment she walked into my living room. We had similar stories and hearts. God knew what He was doing when He put us together. She made some really tough calls on that first book, even telling me the whole thing had to be rewritten. Oh boy, that was a dark day! But she was absolutely correct. She made it a better book—she has made all my books better. I am more than grateful.

I have so many friends who have influenced my thinking about forgiveness. I have had some wonderful discussions on the subject and read countless books. I have had life-changing experiences with forgiveness—how thankful I am for those who did not hold my transgressions against me but showed me God's grace and mercy.

My sweet prayer group who meets monthly at Kathy and Len Hassell's house in Charlottesville to pray for my ministry and me. They bless me in so many ways as they cheer me on. They love me and encourage me and have a deep appreciation for the ministry God has given me. Their prayers lifted Cindy and me over the finish line, and their prayers and sweet friendship continue to carry me as I go out and minister God's grace around the country. I love each dear one.

My dear friends: Dede Hamilton, who generously gave me all her books and material on forgiveness and read the manuscript through to "vet" it for any harshness; I respect her insights; Peggy Garvey, who made sure I took time out to have "fun;" and Tamey Meyer, who keeps my home in order.

And Cindy McCrory, who is my "sister friend." We share a precious friendship—I can tell her anything and know it will not be repeated. No one ever had a better friend.

And my lifelong friends Wynn and Bonnie Lembright. They have lived this journey with me—encouraging, advising, and showing so much love and grace even when I was at my worst. They are deep in my heart.

Russ and Mary Brandes, sweet friends I met through Carson Newman University, let me camp out in their lovely home on Cayman Brac and, along with Nancy and Al Oyer, gave me a "writing nook." I am forever grateful.

Krista Darcus and Michelle Fitzgerald, who keep me organized. They never complain of the tasks I assign but sweetly do them with efficiency and excellence. Both are dear friends.

Without Wayne and Lindsay Williams to keep me in shape after hours sitting at the computer, I would not be upright. I am grateful for their commitment to my physical wellness.

Wes Yoder, my trusted friend and agent. I trust his integrity. His advice is wise and godly. I have deep admiration for him and his staff at Ambassador Speakers Bureau.

And my children, to whom I dedicate this book: Noelle, Graham, and Windsor. I recently told some friends that I have lived long enough to like my kids. They laughed. But to me it was real—there were days I did not like my kids and wondered if I ever would. But I do! They have journeyed with me to a place of forgiveness and joy. It was not easy for them, but their love and forgiveness were never measured. No parent could be prouder of her children than I am of them. And their spouses. Noelle's husband, Maury, and Windsor's husband, Todd, are two very special sons-in-law. They are wonderful men. I could not have asked for better.

My editor, Rebekah Guzman, will never know how her initial response to this insecure author refreshed and encouraged me. And Lissa Halls Johnson, who has such a keen eye and insights. The whole Baker Publishing team has been a joy to get to know and work with—I am delighted to be part of their family. And Lindsey Spoolstra, my project editor, who knows excellence does not demand perfection but wants to get it as close as possible! I am in their debt.

Notes

Chapter 1 Beyond the Prison Walls

1. "It Is Well with My Soul," lyrics by Horatio Spafford (1873), public domain.

Chapter 2 Forgiveness Isn't Fair

1. C. Truman Davis, "A Physician's View of the Crucifixion of Jesus Christ," *CBN*, accessed April 2, 2019, www1.cbn.com/medical-view-of -the-crucifixion-of-jesus-christ.

Chapter 3 God's Heartbeat

1. Paul Thigpen, "Forgiveness: Coming Home to God's Embrace," Bible.org, May 27, 2011, https://bible.org/article/forgiveness-coming -home-gods-embrace.

2. Lewis B. Smedes, *Forgive & Forget* (New York: Harper & Row, 1984), 39.

3. Smedes, *Forgive & Forget*, 39.

4. David Stoop, *Forgiving Our Parents, Forgiving Ourselves: The Definitive Guide*, rev. and updated ed. (Grand Rapids: Revell, 2011), 191.

Chapter 4 The Essence of Forgiveness

1. Sheila Walsh, *The Longing in Me* (Nashville: Thomas Nelson, 2016), 153.

2. Merriam-Webster.com, s.v. "miracle," www.merriam-webster.com /dictionary/miracle.

Chapter 5 The Power of Grace

1. Paul J. Achtemeier, *Harper's Bible Dictionary* (San Francisco: Harper & Row, 1985), 357.
2. Philip Yancey, *Vanishing Grace* (Grand Rapids: Zondervan, 2014), from the preface.
3. Lucinda Secrest McDowell, *Ordinary Graces: Word Gifts for Any Season* (Nashville: Abingdon Press, 2017), 2.

Chapter 6 Choices for the Wounded

1. Greg Ogden, *Discipleship Essentials: A Guide to Building Your Life in Christ* (Downers Grove, IL: IVP Connect, 2007), 10.
2. Merriam-Webster.com, s.v. "reconcile," www.merriam-webster.com/dictionary/reconcile.
3. June Hunt, *Forgiveness: The Freedom to Let Go* (Torrance, CA: Rose Publishing, 2013), 18.
4. Laura Waters Hinson, "Forgiveness on Film," *World Magazine*, July 12, 2008, 20–21.
5. Rick Warren, *The Purpose Driven Life: What on Earth Am I Here For?* (Grand Rapids: Zondervan, 2002), 143.
6. Terry Wardle, *How to Find Wholeness and Inner Healing in Christ* (Abilene, TX: Leafwood, 1994), 35–36.
7. Wardle, *How to Find Wholeness and Inner Healing in Christ*, 35–36.
8. Davis, "A Physician's View of the Crucifixion of Jesus Christ."

Chapter 7 The Call for Help

1. Brennan Manning, *Reflections for Ragamuffins: Daily Devotions from the Writings of Brennan Manning* (New York: HarperOne, 1998), 202.

Chapter 9 Blessings Not Bitterness

1. W. E. Vine, *An Expository Dictionary of New Testament Words* (Old Tappan, NJ: Fleming H. Revell, 1966).
2. *The Revell Bible Dictionary*, s.v. "birthright" (Old Tappan, NJ: Fleming H. Revell Company, 1990), 156.

Chapter 11 Going Backward to Go Forward

1. Merriam-Webster.com, s.v. "despise," https://www.merriam-webster.com/dictionary/despise.
2. Stoop, *Forgiving Our Parents, Forgiving Ourselves*, 130.

3. R. T. Kendall, "How to Forgive Ourselves Totally: Guest Sermon by R. T. Kendall," audio recording, Christ Community Church, Montreat, North Carolina, July 17, 2016, https://stonetablemedia.podbean.com/mobile/e/how-to-forgive-ourselves-totally-guest-sermon-by-rt-kendall/.

4. Kendall, "How to Forgive Ourselves Totally."

5. R. T. Kendall, *How to Forgive Ourselves Totally* (Florida: Charisma House, 2007), 1.

6. Billy Graham, *Just As I Am* (San Francisco: HarperSanFrancisco, 1997), 702.

7. Kurt Strassner, *Opening up Genesis* (Leominster, UK: Day One Publications, 2009), 36.

Chapter 12 What If I Still Can't Forgive?

1. J. Randall O'Brien, *Set Free by Forgiveness* (Cleveland, TN: Parson's Porch Books, 2011), 169.

Chapter 13 Displaying the Character of God

1. R. T. Kendall, *Total Forgiveness* (Lake Mary, FL: Charisma House, 2002), 58.

About Ruth Graham Ministries

Ruth Graham Ministries seeks to motivate people by God's grace and unconditional love from a place of woundedness to a place of wholeness in Christ. Ruth Graham Ministries seeks to create safe places where people can begin their journey to wholeness in Christ.

ruthgrahamministries.org

Facebook: Ruth Graham

Twitter: @RuthBellGraham

BeliefNet: "A Safe Place with Ruth Graham"

About the Authors

Ruth Graham is the author of nine books, including the bestselling *In Every Pew Sits a Broken Heart* and the award-winning *Step into the Bible*. Her passion is to motivate people by God's grace and loving acceptance to move from a place of woundedness to a place of wholeness in Christ. Ruth Graham Ministries seeks to create safe places where people can begin and further their journey to wholeness in Christ. No stranger to heartache, Graham provides a biblical perspective as she shares her journey and points to the faithfulness of God in her own life's heartache. She lives in the Shenandoah Valley of Virginia and has three grown children and nine terrific grandchildren.

Cindy Lambert is a freelance collaborative writer of eleven books including the bestselling *Unplanned* with Abby Johnson. She began her book industry career as owner of an award-winning independent Christian bookstore, then expanded into leadership roles in distribution, consumer research, editorial, and publishing at Ingram, Simon & Schuster, and Zondervan, where she served as vice president and associate publisher of trade books. She currently serves Baker Publishing Group as an executive editor. She and her husband, Dave, have six children and nine grandchildren and enjoy launching their kayaks off their pier in front of their log home in Michigan.

Ruth Graham
MINISTRIES

Ruth Graham Ministries seeks to motivate people by God's grace and unconditional love from a place of woundedness to a place of wholeness in Christ. Ruth Graham Ministries seeks to create safe places where people can begin their journey to wholeness in Christ.

WWW.RUTHGRAHAM.COM

Ruth Graham is represented by Ambassador Literary Agency
Nashville, Tennessee

TO SCHEDULE RUTH TO SPEAK FOR YOUR EVENT,
PLEASE CONTACT: info@AmbassadorAgency.com

 Ruth Graham   @RuthBellGraham

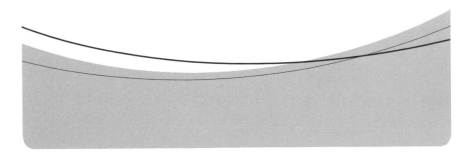